725

p96

NEW IDEAS IN ENVIRONMENTAL EDUCATION

**EUROPEAN YEAR
OF THE ENVIRONMENT**

NEW IDEAS IN ENVIRONMENTAL EDUCATION

EDITED BY
SÁLVANO BRICEÑO AND
DAVID C. PITT

CROOM HELM
London • New York • Sydney

© 1988 International Union for Conservation of Nature and Natural Resources
Croom Helm Ltd, Provident House, Burrell Row,
Beckenham, Kent, BR3 1AT

Croom Helm Australia, 44-50 Waterloo Road,
North Ryde, 2113, New South Wales

Published in the USA by
Croom Helm
in association with Methuen, Inc.
29 West 35th Street,
New York, NY 10001

British Library Cataloguing in Publication Data

Briceño, Sálvano
    New ideas in environmental education.
    1. Environment education.
    I. Title II. Pitt, David C.
    333.7′07   GF26

    ISBN 0-7099-5042-X

Library of Congress Cataloging-in-Publication Data

New ideas in environmental education.

    ''Published in the USA by Croom Helm in association
with Methuen, Inc.'' — T.p. verso.
    Includes index.
    1. Environmental policy — Study and teaching.
2. Environmental protection — Study and teaching.
I. Briceño, Sálvano. II. Pitt, David C.
HC79.E5N45   1987   363.7′007′1   87-15696
ISBN 0-7099-5042-X

**Printed and bound in Great Britain
by Billing & Sons Limited, Worcester.**

CONTENTS

Contents

CONTRIBUTORS

M. Atchia	Chief, Environmental Education & Training Unit, UNEP, P.O. Box 30552, Nairobi, Kenya
K. Boersma	SLO, Dutch National Institute for Curriculum Development, Enschede, The Netherlands
M. Braham	Secretary General, International Association for Integrative Education, 2 rue des Quatre Fontaines, 1261 La Rippe, Switzerland
S. Briceño	Co-ordinator, RCU/UNEP, 14-20 Port Royal Street, Kingston, Jamaica
S. Jakowska	IUCN Commission on Education, Arzobispo Merino 154, Santo Domingo, Dominican Republic
Y. Kakabadse	Executive Director, Fundacion Natura, Casila 243, Quito, Ecuardor
S. Khromov	USSR Academy of Sciences, Moscow, USSR
M.A. Partha-Sarathy	IUCN Commission on Education, "Hamsini", 12th Cross 1, Rajmahal Extns., Bangalore 560 080, India
D.C. Pitt	IUCN, World Conservation Centre, 1196 Gland, Switzerland
J.C. Smyth	Paisley College of Technology, High Street, Paisley, PA1 2BE, UK
V. Sokolov	USSR Academy of Sciences, Moscow, USSR

Contributors

C. Tobayiwa	Mashonaland Wildlife Society, Zimbabwe
D. Variava	Bombay Natural History Society, Bombay, India
J. Voordouw	International Youth Federation for Environmental Studies and Conservation, Klostermollevej 48, 8660 Skanderborg, Denmark
G. Vulliamy	University of York, UK
E. Witoelar	Indonesian Environmental Forum (Walhi), Jakarta, Indonesia

PREFACE

Everywhere in the world there is a demand for 'education', but an uncertainty about what it should mean. 'Much wisdom has eluded us in our efforts to create a sane world'. One message from this book is that often, the wisdom we are looking for is to be found much nearer home, at the grass roots, from the traditions of self-reliance in our villages - and today, because of the telecommunications revolution, the world itself is becoming one village.

The challenge is to combine this village wisdom with the best of science and planning, to make sure that the basic needs of people are met, whilst preserving their environmental heritage. What is required is both evolution as well as radical change, guiding the school system through new avenues, expanding learning, and raising consciousness. It is this synthesis, the combination of the best of the different 'worlds' - old-new, East-West, North-South - which can pave the way towards freedom from deprivation, which seems to be a curse on humanity and this earth.

M.A. Partha Sarathy

ACKNOWLEDGEMENTS

The Editors gratefully acknowledge the assistance and stimulus of the International Environment Education Programme (IEEP) organised by Unesco in cooperation with UNEP. The objectives of this programme are to coordinate and act as a catalyst for national, regional and international activities relative to implementing the recommendations of the Intergovernmental Conference on Environmental Education (Tbilisi, USSR, 1977) including the incorporation of the environmental dimension into education and training programmes, curricula, textbooks and other instructional materials. Readers are recommended to consult the sourcebook - Living in the Environment, Editor in Chief - K.M. Sytnik, Unesco (1985) and the pages presented to the Unesco-UNEP International Congress on Environmental Education (Moscow, USSR, August 1987) which was taking place as this book went to Press. Special thanks are due to Dr. V. Kolybine (Unesco), Dr. M. Atchia and Dr. G. Golubev (UNEP) for advice and support. All authors however write here in their personal capacities.

INTRODUCTION

Sálvano Briceño and David Pitt

This book is a plea for new approaches to environmental education. In recent years there has been an agonising reappraisal of education and a growing awareness of the problems of environment and development. But the two movements have rarely met. Education in the conservation world has been a second class activity and the revolution of ideas about consciousness raising, development from below, and ecodevelopment action have not penetrated far. This is unfortunate because both ideas and actions are moving on rapidly and the conservation organisations run the danger of missing the bus.

Our object here is to present some of the ideas and a sample of the action. This material is put forward for discussion at this time because a major intergovernmental meeting on environment education takes place in 1987, ten years from the famous Tbilisi meeting. Since Tbilisi much water has flowed under the bridge. The ideas put forward there have been widely accepted. But the ecodevelopment problems have increased; more people are living in absolute poverty, there are more environmental disasters, more armaments and threats of war and so on. In the wake of Tbilisi there have been many success stories and some of them are described here e.g. in the USSR (Chapter 4) or in the Third World (Section 2). But these examples are not universal and are limited in time and space. An essential task remains of extending this success and breaking out of the vicious cycles which produce both poverty and conservation problems. We are also suggesting that this liberation requires less new ideas than better means of converting ideas into action including international action.

The scheme of the book reflects this dictum and process. We begin with the frameworks, starting with the ideas which have been extended and elaborated in the last decade. Braham (Chapter 1) sets out the global, humanistic even universalistic paradigms which constitute a holistic ecology including education. What is involved is a new pluralism which embraces all cultures and ideologies. Smyth (Chapter 2) is also a holistic exercise with a bottom-up emphasis dervied from experiences in Scotland. Boersma (Chapter 3), drawing on Dutch reform, tries to clarify precisely what kind of environmental education is needed, especially in schools. Sokolov and Khromov, drawing on Soviet experiences (Chapter 4), point out how environmental education must be in response to specific problems.

But we should remember that change in the formal sector is characteristically slow. Moreover, the Western or perhaps more exactly the Northern tradition is not necessarily appropriate for the South and may be, as Vulliamy shows (Chapter 10), quite counter-productive. Briceno and Pitt (Chapter 6) follow this point by arguing that the World Conservation Strategy and the IUCN should recognise much more not only education but the need to work from below, recognising the potential of the grass-roots and tradition to provide knowledge for meeting basic needs and self-reliance as well as the fundamental importance of informal learning modes.

A reformed system is only part of the solution. There is a need for retrained people to carry forward both new ideas and a broadminded approach which allows constant innovation and adaptability to what are often fast changing situations. There is a need to educate an elite, not least because unless the decision-makers are reached there is unlikely to be either the political will, or the resources, or the legislative authority needed to precede change and to complement a popular will, however strong. In all this the young are central, not only because they are the recipients of most education, but also because they have a futuristic vision and a healthy scepticism of adult rhetoric as well as a proclivity for action and a distaste for inertia. Voordouw (Chapter 5) makes these points from a long experience in youth movements for conservation by particularly emphasising the essential dynamics of open learning and team working.

The other side of the coin are the action situations where endogenous progress is taking place, especially, we should note, in the Third World. Our second second contains discussions of and generally from the Third World. Here we are suggesting a reversal of the normal processes of planning, where ideas and operational outlines come from outside. We are saying we have much to learn from what is happening at what is ethnocentrically called the periphery, and that we need to construct future ideas from these experiences. Much at the grassroots of course mirrors the concerns at the centre and we might regard these case studies as a parallel, if not more practical commentary on the theoretical discussions presented earlier. But there are many differences too, the most striking of which is the lesser influence of formal schooling.

In general, the Third World has a bad press in environment and education areas. Problems are stressed, crises can be seen everywhere, even catastrophes. Nobody would deny that there are serious ecodevelopment problems or that education, including environmental education, is often weakly developed. All this gloom, however, tends to obscure positive phenomena, even a revolution in some Third World settings. The revolution is based on new ideas but also indigenous, even traditional, values which may operate in informal ways often outside school and which puzzle outsiders, but which are the means by which Third World people get round a system which continually dominates them. The machine is driven by an enthusiasm and a vitality particularly noticeable amongst young people.

We begin the section where Jakowska writes from the Dominican Republic about the Laurales movement. Her point is that the best mode of education is through unstructured means and social participation in the context of what she calls the 'conservation mystique'. Something similar (but traditional) exists in Zimbabwe where Tobayiwa evocatively describes what he calls the 'midnight classroom' where the essential rules of conservation are learnt outside school and school hours. If there is one sobering thought in the book, it is his comment that 'in many ways school was a place to go when your education was already complete'. If this is true, it is both sad and a challenge for the future. Vulliamy, using his New Guinea experience, shows some of the constraints generally while Atchia, writing from Mauritius, is anxious to put into the schools the most relevant, essential environmnental concepts.

The Dominican and Zimbabwean stories show clearly how motivation is the strong dynamic pushing towards effective conservation learning. This process is then intimately bound up with an initiation into deep social and cultural experiences. The imprint of such experiences is undoubtedly vivid and a major reason why environmental education must be not only culturally relevant but locally based. There it may draw on not only the mystique and the sentiment but also the co-operative organisational structure, which is what Witoelar describes in Indonesia, in the WALHI movement among young people.

We have started with young people in our chronicle of success stories because in many ways they have led the way. In some countries, they have managed to bring the force of the arguments to the notice of those who hold power and even, as in the students manifestations in France or China in 1986, to make governments change course. But in these processes young people have received much encouragement from an enlightened group of adults who are in many countries part of the conservation lobby. This lobby has been a prime force in education, particularly through influencing both public opinion and decision-makers. The story of Silent Valley in India as told by Variava is a good example of how successful a campaign can be in a developing country setting.

The Silent Valley campaign involved the media, and it has often been said the greatest revolution of our times has been in the field of telecommunication. Even the poorest communities now have access to radio at least. This has affected all branches of environmental education, promoting public awareness as well as changing the minds of decision-makers. Yolanda Kakabadse, working for an NGO in Ecuador, Fundacion Natura, has described how a very effective media campaign promoted both better environmental policies and behaviour.

But for all the mystique, the power and the persuasion, and education formal or informal, most progress still seems to come from the grassroots. If the villages of the world could become self-reliant the problems of ecodevelopment might go away, and environmental education no less than food production would be self-sustaining into the future. It is fitting therefore to conclude with the personal statement of M.A. Partha-Sarathy, both a leader in international environmental education and at the same time working humbly with the poorest of villagers in India.

After all this, we have to conclude that the discussion is not ended but open-ended. We hope these materials will contribute to the debate at Tbilisi + 10 and that future work will follow up on the wealth of ideas presented here. We gratefully acknowledge the support of IUCN but emphasise that all contributors write in their personal capacities.

PART ONE

FRAMEWORKS FOR IDEAS AND ACTION

Chapter One

THE ECOLOGY OF EDUCATION

Mark Braham

THE WORLD SYSTEM

Ecology

My title, the 'Ecology of Education', provides what I believe
to be the proper context for any discussion of education: the
infinite and open system we call nature, within which we are
evolving; which is evolving through us, and of which our
planetary life is but one micro-system.

From this standpoint nature is not just something 'out
there' in the form of fields, forests, clouds and stars, but is
also 'here', and each one of us is a part of nature as well. All
that we do is subject to what we understand are its
principles, those that are known, and undoubtedly those that
are unknown as well.

With all due respect to green politicians, green economists and Greenpeace, ecology is far more than saving
trees, rabbits, dolphins, sites of scenic beauty, and humans
from the ravages of monetarists, vivisectionists, aquatic
zoo-keepers, motorway enthusiasts, power station advo-
cates, and nuclear-weapons testers.

Ecology is nothing less than the study of organisational
reciprocity because every form of life, including our own, is
an organisation in some phase of development or decay, in
constant interchange with its internal and external environment.

Organisation

Organisation is found everywhere both as an all-pervasive
process and as the myriad inorganic, organic and extra-
organic forms that are its products. An organisation is an
inter-relationship of elements, parts or units comprising a
system of behaviour. Every organisation appears at once as
a micro-organisation participating in the creation of an
organisation greater than itself; and as a macro-organisation
dependent upon a hierarchy of micro-organisations from

3

which it derives its existence.

On the one hand, the process of organisation follows a generally regular course of phases and stages of development through which an emerging entity, inorganic, organic or extra-organic, becomes established and self-maintaining in its milieu until it achieves a temporarily optimum state, at which point it either transforms to a higher level of complexity, or becomes relatively fixed in its form and functions, until, according to the nature of its substance and environing conditions, it rapidly, or slowly, decays.

On the other hand, there are the products which emerge out of the process of organisation; molecules are organisations of atoms; organelles are organisations of molecules; cells are organisations of organelles; tissues are organisations of cells; organs are organisations of tissue, and so on throughout the fabric of the flora and fauna of the planet, to human life in its physical, psychological, emotional, perceptual, conceptual, ideational, commercial, industrial, social, political and religious organisation and beyond, such that we can say, 'no organisation, no existence'.

Turning to the opposite direction: while molecules are organisations of atoms, atoms are organisations of electrons, and the neutrons and protons that comprise their nuclei. Neutrons and protons, in turn, are organisations of quarks, and quarks, perhaps, will be found to be made up of yet more minute units, for as the bit of doggerel about fleas says:

> Big fleas have little fleas
> On their backs to bite 'em;
> Little fleas have littler ones
> And so, ad infinitum

Every part - every micro-organisation - acts in a finely articulated and balanced relationship to every other part, from the domains of the infinitely small to the infinitely large; from the infinitely simple to the infinitely complex. A change in any part of a system will, to a greater or lesser extent, affect the whole system.

Reverberations
Hence ecology, for everything exists in a dynamic relationship to everything else. Thus, the present wholesale cutting of trees in tropical moist forests means the destruction of habitats for micro-organisms, insects, birds, animals and people. The loss of foliage means that heavy rains fall

unimpeded on fragile soil whose structure erodes because of lack of root systems to bind it.

The erosion of soil limits plant growth, leading to a loss of humus and the food of bacteria, and thus the food chain is broken until the species that can must migrate or die out - and many do die out - and even the local human population has to leave. The consequences do not stop there, for with the disappearance of the forests oxygen decreases, carbon dioxide increases, and the consequences, subtle and great, reverberate throughout the local, regional, and ultimately planetary eco-system.

The world refugee situation, for example, can be understood in the same ecological context. Instead of insecticides and the well-known consequences of this form of species destruction, bullets, bombs and other kinds of body and mind killing devices are used, forcing some, or even all of the local population to flee and search for another habitat in which to establish a new ecological niche. Often they come into conflict with the indigenous inhabitants who seek to protect the integrity of their own lifestyle. The tensions that result, often leading to rejection or expulsion as they try to gain acceptance and accommodate themselves to and integrate within their new environment, and are common to refugee groups around the world.

Thus, the world ecological problem, largely a human creation, is now working its way out on the human level, and with poetic justice, large numbers of the fleeing populations are seeking - and in some cases are managing to find - asylum in some of the distant countries whose governments, commercial and financial institutions have certain responsibilities for the original disasters.

If the ecological balance of the planet is in disarray, and the evidence for this is available on every continent, the first place to look for causes is within the system itself. There is an obviously lethal factor at work.

As is the case in any organisation when destructive forces emerge - inorganic, organic or extra organic - there is usually something wrong with its information system. In the case of the planetary ecology (and perhaps even the present human propensity for cancer and other severely destructive illnesses) the problem lies in human consciousness. It is human consciousness that has so often been incapable of responding appropriately to the dynamics of life and which lies at the source of the planet's ecological condition.

EDUCATION IS NATURAL

Evolution

While pre-industrial societies were - and to the extent they still exist, are - embedded in nature's seasons and cycles, industrialised and urbanised humanity has been passing through a psychological separation between itself and the rest of nature, acting as if it is the result of some independent and special creation apart from the general evolution of life.

Strange as it may seem, it is only as we have begun to move into the post-industrial, or technological, phase of human life, that this separation is starting to be overcome, and we recognise that we are one among the many species that have evolved on this planet. Whether our evolution is the result of a series of mutations from a progenitor that led on the one hand to the simians, and on the other, to ourselves is still uncertain. We may yet find, as some traditions suggest, that we have come from the stars.

Haekel's old contention, however, that 'ontogeny recapitulates phylogeny' - that is to say, that the development of the individual replicates the evolution of the species (as seen in the formative stages of the human foetus) and the fact of our physical, chemical and biological affinities with other forms of life (as found in trace elements, amino acids, skeletal and tissue structures and functions), suggest that whatever its source or cause, human evolution has long been an intrinsic part of the general evolution of life on this planet.

This evolution is still continuing, but having established the chemical, physical and biological levels of life, it is now to be found working through the dimensions of human emotion, feeling, thought and intuition, and the vast complex of human actions, creations and institutions - and, perhaps, even beyond human life (for who knows that evolution terminates with human kind?).

Information

From the micro-biological end of the evolutionary continuum through to human neuro-physiology, life organises itself on the basis of information that is genetically transmitted from parents to progeny in the course of reproduction. We understand its results as 'instinct'. Because of instinct, the general species type (or genotype) is maintained, but as genes are not exactly replicated during reproduction, distinctive individuals (or phenotypes) emerge, adding their particular characteristics to the gene pool for the inheritance of future generations. Together, genotype and phenotype give rise to both unity and diversity of form, function and behaviour, providing, thereby, for the survival and continuity of species.

Although genetic programming establishes the foundations of individual and species life, it is too limited for the range of behaviour required by highly complex species such as the higher mammals. Of all known species, ours is the most instinctually deficient, while at the same time the most proficient in the complexity, flexibility and refinement of its behaviour.

Maturation
Where genetic programmes exist, we speak of 'maturation' to indicate a generally determined developmental sequence leading from conception to an optimum state, beyond which no major constructive transformations are possible. Amoebae mature, roses mature, cats, dogs and horses mature, their species continue, but, in general, no longer evolve - that is, increase the complexity, flexibility and orderliness of their form, function and behaviour - except to some extent as a result of human intervention.

Although the genetic transfer of information is also a necessary condition for human life, it is largely confined to our neuro-physiological growth and development. Provided that adequate care, food and exercise are available, our bodies mature and achieve the optimum state possible according to the nature of both the internal and external milieux sometime between approximately 23 and 29 years of age. From then on, but for some 'filling out', they will stay in a reasonably recognisable state while ageing, in the form of gradual cellular disorganisation, ultimately takes its toll.

By the same token that our bodies reach maturity, they also do not continue to evolve. Although our species continues to be born, to live and to die in just about all regions of the planet (and now goes for walks and rides in outer space), except perhaps in the case of the fore-brain it has hardly changed, if at all, for thousands of years. Beyond our body's neuro-physiology we do not mature. We cannot achieve maturity.

All that is contained in the ideas of human consciousness, such as our emotional, mental and spiritual life, does not reach maturity. We cannot point to an emotionally, mentally or spiritually mature person, for we know of no final state that marks the criterion of the full flowering of our emotional, mental and spiritual possibilities. In fact, should the present human condition that demonstrates so much discord, violence and destructiveness be the sign of our maturity, we would be in a very sorry situation, as it would signify the limits of what we can become. Fortunately, we are immature, every one of us, and can, therefore, continue to develop and, collectively, can continue to evolve.

The Garden of Eden

The source of our planetary problems lies at that point in evolution at which instinct was transformed to intention through the agency of human life. Like so many events, it is recalled in myth and retold down the ages in the legend of the Garden of Eden.

It was in the Garden of Eden where Adam, our progenitor, was granted dominion over 'the fish of the sea, the fowl of the air, and over every living thing that moved upon the earth', as long as he remained subject to the Will of God. Adam was told that he could partake of everything except the Tree of Knowledge of Good and Evil. Should he eat of that, God said, then 'he would surely die.'

In due course, Eve was created. Then the Serpent appeared and instigated Eve to invite Adam to eat of the fruit of the Tree of Knowledge of Good and Evil. Adam did so, and was cast out of the Garden. From that time on, we are taught, sin entered the world, and has forever been our inheritance.

Some interpretation is in order:

First, the Garden of Eden was Paradise, which, by definition, was perfect - a place of unity and wholeness. In contemporary parlance, some would even call it 'holistic' (which many regard as meaning 'Holy'). It was, however, a setting in which behaviour was pre-determined, ordained by God. As some control system was required to maintain order among the Garden's species, we can suggest, on the basis of our knowledge of genetics, that their behaviour was instinctual, guided by their respective genetic codes.

Second, Adam's behaviour was also prescribed, suggesting that he too, was an instinctual being - possibly as Homo neanderthalis, Neanderthal man - with the locus of his consciousness centered in the hind - or 'instinctual' - brain.

Third, the Serpent, we are told, was 'subtile'. Although

8

in modern Bibles the world subtile is spelled 's-u-b-t-l-e', meaning devious, in the King James' version it is spelled, 's-u-b-t-i-l-e', meaning 'fine, delicate, rarified', something almost ethereal. Traditionally, the Serpent is the symbol of Wisdom, and God's messenger on Earth. Hence, the Serpent symbolises consciousness, a point well understood by yogis and those practitioners who know somewhat of *kundalini*, the 'serpent power', that, rising, through the hierarchy of chakras or centres of consciousness, as they are understood to be in Hindu and Buddhist thought, enables the initiate to acquire successively higher states of awareness.

Fourth, Eve, who is also Isis and Gaia, is the Earth Mother, the feminine principle without whom the power, inherent in matter, of generation and birth would not be possible.

Fifth, as we are dealing with an Asian story that refers back before the Old Testament period, it may be useful to consider that in Sanskrit we find that 'sin', translated as avidya, means 'ignorance', or 'non-knowledge'.

Let us put the story together again:

Adam signifies instinctual man, bound by the then achieved levels of God's creation, who surely did die, as God said he would. The Serpent, as the principle of consciousness, fecundated Eve, the Earth Mother, who in turn, gave rise to a new Adam, a new type of Man, such as Cro-magnon Man, in whom the locus of behaviour had shifted from the hind-brain to include the fore-brain, the seat of reflective thought and from whom modern man, Homo Sapiens sapiens, or 'thinking man', our progenitor, evolved. By eating from the Tree of Knowledge of Good and Evil, Adam broke the bounds of instinct and entered the realm of mind, with its potential for reflection and choice. Once this happened, human life was transformed from instinctual to intentional action, and destiny passed from historical impetus to self-direction.

As is the case with all creation, once the fullness of possibilities has been achieved, and the integrative - or holistic - phase in the organisation of life has been reached in a given milieu, development ceases. For the next phase of development, or for evolution to proceed, a catalyst is required to introduce new information into the system and break the bounds of convention so that transformation can take place.

What then of Adam's sin? Adam did not leave the Garden under a moral cloud, but under an epistemological one. He brought, not evil, but ignorance into the world, for only a non-instinctual being can be ignorant (for the term itself implies an undeveloped capacity for knowledge), and it is this inheritance of ignorance that, to this day, we are still having to expiate.

TEACHING AND LEARNING

Extra Genesis

Ignorance, rather than evil, is our birthright, and wisdom -or 'knowledge integrated through time' as the American philosopher Oliver Reiser defined it - is our possibility. Between the two each generation has to evolve sufficiently to establish a new base of consciousness from which the generation can achieve a little more than its predecessors and, in turn, provide for those who follow. Thus, those modes of response that we roughly categorise as physical, emotional, intellectual, intuitional and spiritual have become interacting stages on the scale of our individual development and collective evolution, and continue to be elaborated, refined and integrated as a part of the 'fine structure' of our planetary life.

It is in the weakness of our immaturity that the strength of our possibilities lie. The lack of genetically transmissible information to underwrite our survival, self-support, and development means that most of the information that is required for the organisation of our lives must be acquired <u>extra-genetically</u>.

Evidence for this is found in the fact that we humans require the lengthiest period of post-natal nurture and guidance until we can become self-supporting. As the amount of information that is required is proportional to the complexity of our culture, this can require up to twelve or thirteen years in 'primitive' societies, and now, up to thirty-five or more years in 'high-technology' nations.

The acquisition of extra-genetic information is what we mean by 'learning'. Although we are instinctively disposed to learn - for our survival depends upon it - we are not born knowing how, or what, to learn. Instead, evolution has provided for more experienced members of the species - parents, family members, others in the local group or community, and finally, those who are especially designated for the task - to be the extra-genetic transmitters of much of the information we require in order to live. Thus 'teaching', 'training' and 'instructing' (recognising that there are significant differences among these), together with learning, take up where instinct has left off in the course of evolution.

Optimising Life

There is more to human possibility, than survival. The overall tendency of every living thing is to optimise its life within its environing conditions. It is this tendency that at the infra-human level provokes maturation and at the human level underlies the search for the fulfilment of possibilities - truth, goodness, beauty and their derivatives - in the impetus for knowledge, creativity, productivity, perfection, happiness and so forth.

Only as successive generations of people are able to elaborate their potentialities and integrate them into programmes of constructive and responsible action can they contribute to the planetary life. It is this collective possibility that is a necessary condition for the continuity of evolution as it works its way through the human dimension.

We should note, however, that the tendency towards what we may call 'optimisation' (the word does not exist in the dictionary) should not be confused with 'aggrandisation'. 'Optimisation' leads to the elaboration of potentialities, as inner resources are tapped, abilities are developed, and the individual is able to offer something to the world. 'Aggrandisation' turns the impetus to optimise into self-interest, acquisitiveness, and possessiveness. It is essentially selfish in its nature and consequence.

For eons human societies have practised division of labour to provide for a more efficient undertaking of necessary skills. The task of assisting the young to learn has thus passed from the immediate and extended family to those specialists whom we call 'teachers'. As in the economy of things a single teacher for a single person is too costly, learners have been gathered and organised into classes and schools, and as social complexity has increased, so have the number, level and programmes of teaching institutions. Thus, we have witnessed the emergence of colleges, universities, and other related establishments in every country and we speak today of the 'educational system'.

But there are questions to be asked:

- to what extent is our family life, the scene of our children's early experiences, educational?

11

- to what extent are our schools, colleges and universities, and other institutions of learning educational?

- to what extent are we, as teachers, lecturers and
  professors, and even as lecturers and professors of
  education, educators?

There is no necessary connection between teaching and
learning and the optimum development of our personal,
local, national and planetary life. We can be - and are -
taught, we can - and do - learn, and we can - and do - teach
others: to be kind and mean; honest and dishonest; harmless
and harmful; creative and destructive; generous and selfish,
and so forth. Teaching and learning can provide for
elaboration of positive human possibilities, or for their
limitation, distortion, and destruction. Neither teaching nor
learning as such are necessarily educational.

The problem is quite straightforward. Although
teaching and learning have their role to play in the extra-
genetic transfer of information, because they are extra-
genetic, they lack an instrinsic criterion. Instead, we apply
extrinsic ones such as examination passes, diplomas and
degrees. But our concern is more than this, it is with that
teaching and that learning that underwrites optimal human
development. Let us reserve the term 'education' for such
teaching and learning and try to give it some substance.

QUALITIES AND TASKS

Qualities of Educational Teaching and Learning
The children and youth and adults presently in schools,
colleges and universities will be the people who will be
responsible for guiding the world in the 21st century.
Hence, the qualities and competencies of consciousness that
will be required depend upon the qualities and competencies
of consciousness we are providing for today.

The Tibetan teacher Dwahl Khul suggests that there are
three aspects to education: Will, Love and Active Intelligence. I believe that we can regard these as necessary
qualities for educational teaching and learning and for our
individual, family, group, community, national and planetary
life. Each quality requires the others and none can function
adequately alone. Together they comprise a daily and
eternal triangle for our work.

Will. Will is nothing less than life's pressure to mani-

12

fest, to develop, to act, as it appears at the human level. Will is concentrated and directed energy - it is active intentionally. Without will we cannot get out of bed in the morning, without will we accomplish nothing: there can be no creative action, no difficulties can be met and overcome, and problems, instead of becoming possibilities, remain obstacles, and potentialities remain inert.

Love. Love is creative entry into the life of the 'other' - the 'not-self'. It recognises and supports the other's tendency to self-realisation - what the psychologist Maslow called the 'press towards fuller and fuller being' - and because it concerns the other, it bestows freedom. Love, therefore, has nothing to do with possessiveness, or attachment, for these refer not to an interest in the other for themselves, but to our self-interest, our needs, our desires, our hopes and aspirations. The Existentialist philosopher, Jean-Paul Sartre, correctly I believe, made the distinction between 'being for others' and 'being for oneself'. Love means 'being for others'.

This approach to love differs from that we normally take, in which we love in what we may call the 'appetite mode' - loving others according to the satisfactions we derive from them, so that they, like a good meal, or a glass of fine wine, are to be tasted, swallowed, digested and enjoyed in order to appease our hunger and satisfy our appetite. As with those dishes that we regard as no longer delectable, we often push the unsatisfying one away like a plate of cold cabbage.

Active Intelligence. By active intelligence, we can understand the development and use of mind in its analytical or discriminative function on the one hand, and its synthesising or discriminative function on the other, and both in their intellectual, technical, or artistic modes. In contemporary terms it involves the ability to translate sensory and even extra-sensory messages into information, to transform information into concepts, ideas and theories, beliefs, and where possible knowledge, which, in turn, can be applied to the intentional organisation of life.

Will without love and intelligence lacks sensitivity and discrimination, and results in blind and forceful action that distorts and destroys.

Love without knowledge and will is a misnomer, as it is really sentimentality, of comfort, perhaps, to the self, but lacking creative effect upon the other, the not-self.

Intelligence without love becomes divisive, manipulative, and even destructive; for it can never understand or know the other; without will it remains inert, undeveloped and inapplicable.

Translated into teaching:

Will implies teaching that is vital, committed, and directed towards providing for the fullest possible development of the human potential for creative action.

Love implies caring about those who are being taught, what is taught and how it is taught.

Intelligence implies the development and application of all of the mental abilities that we can bring to bear upon the act of teaching.

Collectively these three qualities create not only a dynamic setting for education, but involve us as teachers in our own continuous self-transformation as willing, loving and actively intelligent people.

Translated into learning:

Will engages the initiative of pupils and students and transforms love and intelligence into purpose. The concept of docility, so useful under pedagogical regimes in which authority rather than educational leadership is marked, provides less for the optimal development of the person than it does for passivity, and the reactions of disillusionment and even violence.

Love encourages each pupil and student to recognise their own worth, and the worth of each other; to care about their learning; and to join will and intelligence into caring for the planet - the ultimate recipient of their attitudes and actions.

Intelligence implies the development of reflectiveness, discrimination, critical analysis and constructive synthesis, engaging all of the capacities of the brain to unify the intellectual, aesthetic, and intuitive features of the mind, to give direction to will, qualified by love.

Four Tasks

The process of education involves each of us as learners in at least four main tasks[1]:

(a)   adaptation to the environment;
(b)   participation in the environment;
(c)   creative contribution to the environment;
(d)   constructive transformation of the environment.

(a)   Adaptation to the environment largely concerns

14

infancy, and the 'fittingness' of the individual to his surroundings. The human infant, like the young of all species, is a dependent being who must be cared for. His earliest activities basically concern his survival in a post-uterine state, and the differentiation and integration of his total organic system.

While the child's adaptive behaviour patterns begin below the threshold of cognition, by his first year his activities show considerable self-determination. During the first four or five years of his life the child, under the direction and guidance of parents, and members of the immediate - and, where existing, the extended - family learns what and how to eat and dress, to speak and understand the local language, and to comprehend and respond to the expectations of an increasing number of people. He begins, in sum, to identify with, and to acquire, his culture. In whatever manner it is brought about, the child's ability to adapt to his environment is a necessary condition of any further development.

(b) Participation in the environment belongs essentially to middle and later childhood. It concerns children's engagement in activities which, for the most part, are conducive to maintaining the society. While adaptation continues to be a concern of the individual, it is far from all that is required. Adaptation is essential autocentric, or egocentric, for it essentially concerns the individual's need to survive. Participation is essentially allocentric, or sociocentric, as it concerns the society to which the child has had to adapt.

(c) Creative Contribution to the environment belongs to adolescence. The evolution of a society rests upon the development of its members, and this means that they must be able to contribute in ways that take it beyond the status quo. The problem is that our school programmes concentrate on shaping the young for social adaptation and participation, but devalue creative and innovative learning. Thus, time and again, the creativity of our societies has rested in the hands of a very small minority who have been able to succeed despite, rather than because of, their institutions.

By creative contribution we may understand the application of novel responses to continuing or new circumstances, such that these responses become part of the general fabric of the society, and provide for an improvement over the normal patterns of thought and action. This implies that there is more to creativity than merely a spontaneous or novel response to a new situation. Creativity emerges when it becomes organised and directed towards the solution of problems and to the elaboration of new possibilities of human life, whether we are dealing with artistic, literary, philosophical, scientific, political, legal, technical or other features.

Creativity thus must be grounded in a recognition of the cultural conditions within which it is to be applied. This requires the ability to objectify, and reflect upon, the conditions of life, something that is scarcely possible before adolescence, yet which during adolescence can focus attention upon prevailing conditions and new possibilities, which then form the framework for entry into responsible adulthood.

Except in rare cases, therefore, we would not expect to find culturally contributive activity emerging much before middle or later adolescence. Hence, while the impulse to innovate and create is certainly available and requires support throughout childhood, we must turn to adolescence and to secondary schooling as the locus for guiding creative talent into culturally contributive activities.

(d) Constructive transformation of the environment is that action which experience and reflection suggest will provide for the overall improvement of life. But unless the members of a society have been prepared to be constructively transformative, and achieve the competency to conceive and carry out constructive activities, we are liable to find but change for the sake of the changers, and not necessarily for justifiably conceived purposes. While in adolescence we find the 'birth' of objective and reflective thought, it is unlikely that one will find the intellectual proficiency that enables the rational search for alternatives. Rather, this is really a feature of education at the early adult level, and a responsibility of colleges and universities.

THE CONTENT OF EDUCATION

Contemporary Crises

Unless we have a particularly pathological inclination to indulge ourselves in the darker side of life, we prefer to avoid the fact of crises. Whatever they are, we either wish that they will go away, or that someone will resolve them for us. We are little inclined to accept crises as an impetus for the constructive transformation of life. But we cannot transform life without facing the crises, noting their causes and consequences, conceiving solutions and reorienting our lives accordingly.

There are at least five categories of crises:

The Physical Crisis, exemplified by the breakdown of the planetary ecology as a consequence of pollution and the destruction of human and non-human life and habitats; over-population and poverty in many countries; continuing warfare; the plight of refugees; and unemployment.

The Psycho-Social Crisis, exemplified by the high incidence of psycho-somatic and general psychological illnesses; drug dependence and abuse; marriage breakdowns, and personal and civil violence.

The Aesthetic Crisis, exemplified by the separation of much in the contemporary arts from ordinary human experience and meaning; the degradation of urban areas in many nations, and an overall lack of poise, balance and harmony in our daily life.

The Intellectual Crisis, exemplified by the proliferation of technological and scientific knowledge that is beyond general comprehension; the lack of moral competence to guide it, and irrationality and anti-intellectualism on the part of many people who find little satisfaction in developing their mental possibilities.

The Spiritual Crisis, exemplified by the sense of irrelevance in the practices of traditional religious institutions and a widespread search for new spiritual realities.

Most of these crises are of our own making. They are expressions of the quality and content of our consciousness - of our awareness, attitudes, interests, knowledge, understanding and values. As such they indicate the need for our schools, colleges, universities and other teaching and learning institutions to reconsider their programmes and practices so that they can fulfil their roles as agents between the person and the planet.

The Physical Dimension
Any programme of education must be directed towards overcoming the sense of separation between human and non-human life. This must include developing a sense of care for, and responsibility towards, the rest of nature. Animal husbandry, horticulture, agriculture, and wildlife conservation are a means for understanding growth processes, the

principles that govern them, and how, as humans, we actively fit into the scheme of life. Appropriate technology for the use, for example, of wind, water and solar power has its place, along with the acquisition of such basic skills as carpentry, plumbing, masonry, painting and decorating, household care and food preparation.

These should not be seen as a subject for the less academic, or more mechanically or technically inclined, but as a part of a general curriculum concerned with building the foundations of a responsible consciousness. The overall result should be an increased competence in the reciprocal living with others and the rest of nature that our planetary life requires.

The Psycho-Social Dimension

While our separation from the rest of nature is a problem within the physical dimension of our lives, our separation from one another is equally a problem. Although there are many examples around us of sensitive and compassionate living, we are also faced with patterns of reactive, hostile and destructive behaviour in ourselves, and in our family, group, professional and organisational life. These are also to be found on the highest levels of commercial, industrial and governmental decision-making, whether local, national or international.

Schooling should provide each person with the opportunity to become more aware of themselves and of others through sharing in common work, study, concerns and responsibilities. A community approach that provides for collaborative living without the loss of personal identity or individuality is vital.

As positive personal development often needs supportive guidance, there is an important role to be played by sensitive counselling psychologists, whose concern, which should also include academic development, must be for the optimum development of the consciousness of child, adolescent or adult. This seems to be an approach most appropriately undertaken from the standpoint of the transpersonal psychologies that emphasise our ability to understand the various 'sub-personalities' that govern and often negatively restrict our lives, and the 'higher self' that can be the source of productive living.

The Aesthetic Dimension

The energies of life run in two directions: aesthetically, an increase in the organisation, integration and flexibility of both form and function - harmony, order and unity - on the one hand; unaesthetically, as disorganisation, disintegration, inflexibility, imbalance - disharmony, disorder, and disunity - on the other. The first concerns evolution and development; the second, involution and destruction.

This aesthetic tendency is to be found in the structure of molecules and cells, of plants and flocks of birds, and in the movement even of the planets. It is expressed in the balanced swing of a wood-cutter's axe; in the economy of motion of a peasant's scything; and even in the rhythm of machines, where lack of rhythm is the sign of a fault. Rites and rituals; music, dance and drama; poetry and prose; design, craft and art; the scientist's and mathematician's search for 'beautiful solutions' and 'elegant proofs' signify the place of the aesthetic in our lives.

Among other forms of life aesthetic expression is instinctual. For ourselves, it must be learned. Without it, we are unable to create. Because any education that is worthy of the name is an aesthetic education, opportunities for working in a wide range of arts and crafts are essential, not as an added extra, nor a 'soft option', but as a vital and valid part of learning.

The Intellectual Dimension
We are aware of the importance of paying care and attention to the details of our physical life. We are rapidly becoming aware of this necessity in our emotional and social life. Aesthetic expression also requires it. Despite, however, the sophistication of many school, college and university programmes, we tend to forget the importance of paying care and attention to our thought-life, except perhaps for limited academic and employment purposes. We seldom realise that our thoughts have a certain 'tangibility', that they are the way we 'map' the world and create our individual and collective reality. We tend to neglect the fact that our thoughts have effects, containing consequences for ourselves and others, whether spoken, written or stored at some level of our consciousness.

As so much of the intellectual work in schools is limited to the attempt to acquire good examination results, diplomas, degrees and successful employment, under intensively competitive conditions, large numbers of potentially capable students are discouraged from 'using their minds'. In reaction to what is often felt to be the

19

'soulless' nature of learning, it has become fashionable even among successful students to deny the importance of thought and a developed intelligence.

Consequently, in the present period in which traditional patterns or beliefs are being shattered and little that is stable is taking their place, most adults, not having been provided with the encouragement and support to marshal their mental energies to take them beyond the concrete level on which most everyday activities are carried out, lack the strength of clear and intelligence purpose upon which to base their individual and collective living.

The work of secondary and post-secondary education must include opportunities for exploring, and reflecting upon the fundamental ideas that have shaped contemporary life, provide a background for understanding the present world crises, and enable us to comprehend something of the nature of man, and our place in nature.

There is the need for students to engage in an individual and collaborative search for practical alternatives that can help to transform the planetary condition, particularly as these concern ecological, environmental, economic, employment, political and social issues. It is only as learning becomes intellectually alive, as it can touch the 'growing age' of thought in the arts, sciences and humanities, and can be applied to life, that we can encourage students to accept the responsibilities of their impending adulthood.

The Spiritual Dimension

Our time is one that is marked by a spiritual quest. Although there has been a loss of faith in traditional religious practices, and little satisfaction in the secularity of the past decades, there is a widespread search for meaning that may include, but cannot be satisfied by, ordinary rationality.

For some people in the West, at least, this quest means turning to the roots - to the spirit, rather than to the letter - of the Judaic-Christian teachings. Other have turned to different traditions: Hinduism, Tibetan and Zen Buddhism, Taoism or Sufism, for example. Others again are searching along that ancient stream of thought that ran through the Egyptian, Green and Roman Mystery Schools, and continued with the Gnostics, Cathars, Templars, Freemasons, Cabbalists, Rosicrucians, alchemists, Theosophists, Anthroposophists and a number of less know but not less important groups.

Whichever path is chosen, some common experiences

are ultimately recorded: 'expansions of consciousness' that bring with them 'peak experiences' or 'higher' levels of awareness. These call for, and assist, the integration of our physical, emotional and mental life. They gradually release us from the incessant claims of the personality and its self-interest. In time a sense of unity with, and a responsibility towards, the evolution of life is found. The seeker may experience what is called a 'state of grace', a sense of 'union with God', 'cosmic consciousness', *samadhi, satori* or whatever term is appropriate to a given path.

We should recognise the validity of this quest. We cannot, however, nor should we attempt to, indicate to anyone what should be their spiritual path. Both the search and the attainment are personal matters. We should, however, provide opportunities for each student to explore some of the 'ways of realisation' through the study and practice of some of the major spiritual disciplines.

Craftsmanship

This may appear to be an odd item to include under the 'Content of Education', but it belongs here as an essential constituent of any process worthy of the name of education. Although it may seem to be a very mundane matter, craftsmanship is nothing less than the application of care and attention to the detail of all aspects of one's work. Without attention to detail, the greatest aspirations remain left in a cloud-bank of ideas, because the quality of work rests not just upon the breadth of vision that instigates it, but upon the attention we give it to its smallest detail. It only requires a crack in a minute jewel to stop the finest watch; a misplaced comma to bring a computer program to a halt; or a missing bolt to bring an aircraft crashing down through the sky. It is the old story of battles being lost for the want of a horseshoe nail.

Craftsmanship involves both attitude and skill; attitude is the psychological condition, skill is the technical one. Where there is no caring attitude, skilfulness is lacking. Where there is not skilfulness, the quality of work, and by extension the quality of personal, social and national life, are restricted.

A part of the tedium of school life in earlier decades was the often boring and repetitive attention to such communication skills as spelling, punctuation, grammar and even speech. For the most part these were treated as if they were of value in and of themselves quite apart from their usefulness or any interest a learner might have in them. It was as if, for example, one should learn how to lay bricks simply for the sake of laying bricks. Similar examples could be found in a range of fields where learning the skills were almost a prerequisite to entering into the substance of the subject - the fine arts were a major example. This resulted in the stifling of creative interests and talent. It was an expression of the idea, still held by many people, that education is 'preparation' for life, rather than being a part of the dynamic of life itself.

Eventually, a change of emphasis appeared with the understanding that as the function of a skill is to permit a task to be performed - we learn how to lay bricks in order to build walls and houses - skills are best learned in the course of learning the substantive field in which they are to be applied. All well and good, the tedium of learning isolated techniques was removed as student became more involved in the substance of their subjects.

As attention to substance learning increases, however, attention to skill learning tended to decrease, with the consequences of loss of quality which has led to increasing concern about a general carelessness, for example, in literacy and numeracy among secondary school students and adults, with a consequent demand for a return to 'basics': reading, writing and arithmetic as they used to be taught.

This demand, in turn, has given rise to what can be called process ideology. The idea here is that it is not so much what one produces that counts, as it is the experience of the process, and further, that a demand for a well-produced product, whether an essay, a piece of music or a painting, is liable to stifle initiative.

As is probable with all dichotomies, this separation of process from product is a false one as it does not take into account that the quality of the process establishes the quality of the product, and that the quality of the product establishes both a technical and a psychological reference point for the further processes that we undertake. Thus, if the process is what really counts in learning, why bother to be concerned about the quality of one's products? It is not too difficult to image the effect that this attitude has on the productivity of a nation in general when students take it into their working lives.

The need for skilfulness is not just limited to 'school subjects', but involves the whole gamut of our lives: the quality of our dealings with our environmnent; our relationships with one another; and our commercial, industrial, technological, scientific and professional activities. Skilfulness in the tools of our trades, whether these are tools of the hand, the heart, or of the mind, is as essential to education as is the subject matter itself.

NOTES ON THE EDUCATION OF TEACHERS

The Profession of Teaching

Our requirement, then, is for that learning and that teaching that we can call educative. Our concern is to place education in its proper context as a primary means for the evolution of human consciousness and, therefore, to enable all of those who would regard themselves as 'educators' to recognise that their responsibility includes the person, the planet-at-large - and, given the present forays into 'outer space', it may well be time for them to contain the universe in their thoughts as well.

One of the most important gateways to educational change is that of teacher education. One of the first problems that has to be faced is the fact that in many countries, teachers have been seen first as more or less qualified child-minders, and then as technicians whose job is to prepare children and youth 'for life'. 'Life' is generally understood as that which satisfies the interests of the dominant elite within the society, interests which are usually conservative in nature. Teachers are seen, therefore, not so much as professionals, but as pedagogical civil servants.

In English-speaking countries, in particular, teachers have not enjoyed high regard. Their remuneration is generally lower, and the quality and content of their preparation is less rigorous than in other professions. Additionally, the commitment of many people who become teachers is less to being professional educators, than to being able to have a job in the face of not knowing what else to do. Hence the well-worn adage that:

> Those who can, do;
> Those who can't do, teach;
> Those that can't teach, teach teachers.

I am happy to exclude from this description that untold number of highly intelligent, skilled and dedicated teachers who care about their work, and do so with incredible tenacity under conditions that are often as perverse as they are almost insuperable. Yet the fact remains, that the teaching profession is not one of the brightest stars on the human horizon. Too many teachers, for too long, have been reduced to having to be concerned about job security, adequate pay and pension rights, rather than, if they were properly selected, prepared and paid, being able to attend to the profession of education.

Outlines of a Programme

An appropriate programme of teacher education must regard the qualities and competence required of teachers as among the highest needed by any society. This is not a matter of pious aspiration but the recognition that human consciousness is the vital factor upon which the development of nations ultimately depends.

Despite the distinctiveness of each person, and the different rate at which each develops, the quality of individual consciousness is inseparable from the quality of teaching each has received. And the quality of teaching is inseparable from the quality of the teachers.

Hence, we must regard good teachers as one of the most valuable of our human resources, and both provide for, and require of them, the highest competence that we can conceive. Potential teachers must find their preparation amidst the most intelligent of the population in the best institutions a nation has to offer.

Given the historical fact that colleges, and even university departments, of education have long been cast into the role of academic second-class citizens, rather than attempt to change them, it might be best to dispense with them for the purposes of teacher education. There is a role, however, for inter-disciplinary centres of advanced studies in education.

Instead, let all teacher preparation take place within the universities, requiring of potential teachers that they meet the same qualifications as other university students. At the same time the universities should be required to accept responsibility for the development of the nations' education. In suggesting this I fully recognise that our universities are also not exempt from the need to deal, radically in many cases, with their programmes and teaching methods. But this requires a further discussion.

A programme of teacher education should cover at least four years. Intending teachers should undertake both an interdisciplinary base of subjects that bear directly upon the process of education, as well as the subject of their proposed teaching fields. Courses such as philosophy, history, and sociology of education, along with educational psychology, for example, should be taught by the substantive departments.

If the normal organisation of degree programmes in universities makes it difficult to integrate students intending also to be teachers, the successful experience with programmes of independent studies suggests that it should not be too difficult for each student to organise, with the assistance of a capable tutor, an individualised programme appropriate to his or her concerns.

Each university should also have a 'Centre of Educational Services'. The task of the Centre staff will be to accept, guide and monitor each student through an apprenticeship programme in local schools to begin in the student's first year.

During their first year, students should spend a number of hours per week as 'teaching aides' assigned to practicising teachers. This will give the students the opportunity to determine whether or not they are suited for teaching.

If it is agreed that a student should not pursue a teaching career he or she should be able to continue in the university, without penalty, towards obtaining a degree in a field of study. As long as they are able to maintain their academic work, the option to withdraw from teaching while being able to continue as degree students should hold for their full period of university studies.

During their second year, students should become 'assisting teachers', with responsibilities for teaching certain aspects of lessons, or groups of pupils under the supervision of class teachers.

In their third year, students should become 'associate teachers' under the supervision of class teachers, but with more independence and responsibility for teaching a specific subject.

In their fourth year, students should continue their 'associate teacher' status, but with full responsibility for a given subject area under the normal supervisory structure followed by the rest of the staff. In large schools there should, anyway, probably be a senior staff member assigned to co-ordinate the apprenticeship programme.

At the end of their four years, students will have had to successfully complete both their academic and internship requirements in order to obtain their university degree and teaching certificate.

Students who have not successfully completed their teaching internship, but have successfully completed their academic work, would still be entitled to their degree without prejudice. If, however, any students fail their degree work they will also not be able to receive their teaching certificate. Such an approach means that new teachers will start their full-time work as qualified professionals, competent both in teaching and in an appropriate field of study.

Although it was argued in the past that the need for teachers far outweighed the numbers available, so that setting higher standards would drastically reduce the number needed, the situation is now quite different. I suspect that it will be found that given changing employment patterns (and unemployment) there is a considerable reservoir of potential talent ready to undertake teacher preparation to enable us to transform a pedagogical civil service into a highly skilled teaching profession.

NOTES ON EDUCATIONAL OPPORTUNITY

There is a saying attributed to the Chinese philosopher Kuan-Tzu:

> If you plan for a year, plant rice;
> If you plan for ten, plant trees;
> If you plan for one hundred years,
> Educate mankind.

Educational opportunity is not a right, nor a privilege, but a matter of natural necessity. Without it, the development of individual consciousness is restricted, as is the consciousness of families, groups and nations. And where the potencies of love, intelligence and will that are latent in each person are left unawakened and unapplied to the whole range of human endeavour, there can hardly be a constructive transformation of the planet.

Educational opportunity should not be seen as a steeple-chase, where only the best manage to win, with the laurels of society bestowed upon them, while those who are not the 'front-runners' are farmed out as unworthy, or left, as too many youth and adults are today, under-educated, unemployed, or if employed, without the possibility of expanding their horizons of ability.

Educational opportunity is the means whereby as broad a base of talent as possible can be encouraged for its application to the life of nations. But even more, it is only through educational opportunity that the consciousness of the individual can transcend those stages of consciousness that have been slowly worked out through the eons of human experience.

The overall dynamic of human evolution has given rise to - as well as resulting from - a hierarchy of stages of consciousness that are potentially available to each person. The movement has been uneven, it has not taken place to the same extent everywhere, or at the same time. Looked upon globally, despite the fact that our vision is often obscured by the confusion of human behaviour, the overall thrust is clear:

From a base in essentially physical-plane activity as seen, for example, in hunting and gathering, agriculture, mining and construction; to the plane of emotions with its swings of reactivity and desire, as seen in the violence of wars and passions of the heart (think of the paradox of the love for God and the hatred of man that has taken priest-blessed banners into battles); to the true plane of the heart with the emergence of compassion and love (note, for example, how recently it is in human history that life has been regarded other than as cheap, and the 'caring professions' such as nursing and social work have appeared on the scene); to the explorations of mind, and the spread of literacy, the arts, humanities, the sciences and technology, until finally, in our day, increasing numbers of people are focussing their attention on human spiritual possibilities, rather than leaving these as the prerogatives of members of religious orders.

This has been no simple and upward linear movement, but rather, a gradual change in emphasis, so that while some of the most ancestral of human activities are still with us (for example, repressive dictatorships, the savagery of warfare, and the infamy of torture) increasing numbers of people join in the forward flow, and in each generation, what has been encountered on the borderland of new possibilities has been used to transform the traditional patterns.

It has not only been the metals of weapons that have been used to make many a ploughshare and a pruning hook, but today's science and technology is beginning to help us understand the ways of the 'fish of the sea, the birds of the air, the cattle, and every creeping thing that creeps upon the earth', and our quest for knowledge is leading us to begin righting the wrongs of generations of human misuse of human and non-human life. Even the realms of the spirit are having their effect as more and more healers are assisting doctors to cure the sick, and the inner mysteries of the great religious traditions are providing a reorientation to a new spiritual view of life. The higher must always serve the lower, that the lower may arise and find its way to the higher, as Jesus taught by washing the feet of the Disciples.

Gradually, all the changes are being rung, as each centre of human consciousness from the physical to the spiritual is somewhere sounding out on the planet, so that it is not too much to say that humanity is gradually transforming the very sound and timbre of the planet itself.

What has this to do with 'educational opportunity'? Everything. Every new advance of human possibility finds its way back into society-at-large through some process of teaching and learning. Whether the teaching is by direct experience - showing someone a better way to pump water, or to till the land - or whether it is through an apprentice beating out and engraving silver under the watchful eyes of a master smith; or as a result of a group of young students listening, questioning, discussing with their teacher, or of older adults searching for new ideas in whatever field, there is teaching, and learning of some kind, and to some extent. To the extent that teaching and learning lead towards the optimum development of life, then there is education.

We acquire our entry into the next realm of consciousness, usually because someone has either been there before us and opened a door, or helped us sufficiently until, skilled in the task, we can even bypass our teachers and open our own doors. And having opened them, we can then help others to open theirs, and even to bypass us, in their quest of the next step ahead.

What are the limits? There are none, other than potentiality, volition and opportunity. Yes, there are those whose bodies so restrict them that hand, heart and mind cannot fully function, yet even they, at every level of incapacity, have their own learning to undertake and lives to lead. Far more, however, are the vast numbers of people who have the potentiality, but not the possibility, which they could have if the resources, encouragement and guidance to enable them to discover themselves and their world would be provided.

It is not a matter of sweetness and light to talk about

lifelong learning. It is a matter of the evolution of human consciousness, which cannot be limited to a few years of childhood, adolescent and young adult schooling, with each year being like the sides of an enclosing pyramid, allowing fewer and fewer to move upwards. It would be far better to establish systems of education that open the world to human possibility, and human possibility to the world.

In the words of Pierre Teilhard de Chardin:

> The outcome of the world, the gates of the future, the entry into the super-human - these are not thrown open to a few of the privileged, nor to one chosen people to the exclusion of all others. They will be open to an advance of all together, in a direction in which all together can join and find completion in a spiritual renovation of the earth ...

The Phenomenon of Man

POSTCRIPT

I am well aware that I am open to the charge of 'woolly idealism' particularly as I have not demonstrated the practical implications, in programmatic terms, of many of the ideas in this paper. Without wishing to avoid the issue, there really is not the space here to elaborate the details.

If the charge is meant to imply that I am simply offering counsels of perfection that do not take into account the everyday realities the work of teachers and present financial conditions, let me reply as follows:

Teachers - and not just those in the 'inner cities', but also in suburbs and towns across the country (I exclude, for the present, the independent or private school sector, which requires another discussion) - are facing almost insurmountable odds in terms of student reaction (as one headmaster stated it, many students are simply 'voting with their feet', and are staying away), long hours, oversized classes, insufficient resources, simply bad working conditions and a lack of political will to bring about the needed changes.

But this does not alter the fact that a fundamental revising of our pedagogical thoughts and practices to make them truly educational is required. We need a new vision for education, one that is appropriate for this end of the century, in order to build for the century to come.

If I have presented ideals, it is because ideals are those

processes and products that are conceived to do a job more effectively than it is otherwise being done. There is nothing ideal about having a ham-fisted surgeon, or setting out on a long trip in a dilapidated car that tends to break down every few miles. As such, ideals are practical; inadequacy and inefficiency are not. And that which is practical, which is that which works best, is the ideal and the most realistic.

There is nothing ideal, practical or realistic in continuing those pedagogical arrangements that limit the human potential, and continue behaviour patterns which mark the darker side of the human condition. As a final comment, let me add the thoughts from some ancient wisdom:

> If you don't keep an eye
> on the mountain peak,
> your feet
> can't
> follow
> the
> path.

NOTES

1. This is a revised version of a lecture given at the 'Education in the 21st Century' conference, held at the Findhorn Foundation, Forres, Scotland, at the beginning of April 1986.

   I must thank Austin Arnold, that continual stimulator of projects and ideas who helped to instigate the conference, for raising the point with me one traffic-jammed morning about the primacy of teachers in the development of a nation's human capital.

   Thanks, too, to Caro Hall and Michael Lindfield of the Findhorn Foundation for their invitation, and to the members of the Foundation for providing the setting and a knowledge about the inner side of education from which the world of teaching can benefit.

   Claude Curling, formerly Sub-Dean of Sciences at King's College, University of London, Janice Dolley of the Open University in England, and Dr. Walid Kamhawi, President of the al-Quds Open University Project, Amman, Jordan, made a number of appreciated comments towards the revision of the original text.

BIBLIOGRAPHY

Assagiolo, Roberto, Psychosynthesis, New York, Hobbs, Dorman, 1965.

Attar, Farid-udin, The Conference of Birds, trans. by C.S. Nott, London, Routledge & Kegan Paul, 1985.

Allport, Floyd H., Theories of Perception and the Concept of Structure, New York, Wiley, 1955.

Bailey, Alice A., Education in the New Age, London, Lucis Publishing Company, 1954.

_____ The Light of the Soul: The Yoga Sutras of Patanjali, London, Lucis Publishing Company, 1927.

Braham, Mark, Natural Organisation and Education, unpublished Ph.D. dissertation, Stanford, California, Stanford University, 1972.

_____ 'Education is Natural', in M. Braham, ed., Aspects of Education, Chichester, UK, John Wiley, 1982.

_____ The Centre for Integrative Education, Geneva, International Association for Integrative Education, 1985.

Buber, Martin, Between Man and Man, London, Routledge & Kegan Paul, 1947.

Darlington, C.D., The Evolution of Man and Society, London, George Allen & Unwin, 1969.

Dobzhansky, Theodozius, Mankind Evolving, New Haven, Yale University Press, 1962.

Goudge, T.A., The Ascent of Life, Toronto, University of Toronto Press, 1961.

Handler, P., ed., Biology and the Future of Man, New York, Oxford University Press, 1970.

Hayward, Jeremy, Perceiving Ordinary Magic, Boulder, Colo., USA, Shambhala, 1984.

Huxley, Julian, Evolution, the Modern Synthesis, New York, Wiley, 1964.

_____ Evolution in Action, New York, New American Library, 1973.

Jaynes, Julian, The Origin of Consciousness and the Breakdown of the Bicameral Mind, London, Allen Lane, 1976.

Jung, C.G., Modern Man in Search of his Soul, New York, Harper, 1933.

Lazslo, Ervin, The Systems View of the World, New York, George Braziller, 1972.

Lovelock, J.E., Gaia, Oxford University Press, 1979.

John Macmurray, The Self as Agent, London, Faber & Faber, 1957.

31

Merleau-Ponty, Maurice, The Structure of Behaviour, Boston, Beacon Press, 1963.

Nasr, Sayed Hossein, Man and Nature, London, George Allen & Unwin, 1968.

Piaget, Jean, The Child's Conception of the World, Patterson, New Jersey, Litlefield Adams, 1963.

_____ Six Psychological Studies, New York, Random House, 1967.

Sheldrake, Rupert, Morphogenic Fields, London, Anthony Blond, 1985.

Sinnott, Edmund Ware, The Biology of the Spirit, New York, Viking, 1955.

_____ Cell and Psyche, New York, Harper, 1961.

Teilhard de Chardin, Pierre, The Phenomenon of Man, London, Collins, 1961.

Waddington, C.H., Tools for Thought, London, Granada, 1977.

_____ Towards a Theoretical Biology, Chicago, Aldine, 1968.

Werner, Heinz, The Comparative Psychology of Mental Development, New York, Science Editions, 1961.

Whitehead, Alfred North, Process and Reality, New York, Macmillan, 1929.

Chapter Two

WHAT MAKES EDUCATION ENVIRONMENTAL?

J.C. Smyth

During the past ten years we have seen a remarkable growth of interest in our environment and in the need for people, especially young people, to learn about it. There have been many exciting ideas and many successes, as this book reveals. They have been most evident in the informal sector, under the inspiration of out-of-school organisations, or in the more elementary levels of the formal sector, and most of the new materials produced as teaching aids have reflected this.

In many countries penetration of the secondary level of formal education has been less easy, and this is unfortunate since 'serious' education tends to be measured by its usefulness as the means of entry, through qualifying examinations, to higher education and employment. Here traditional subjects with long-established philosophies still hold sway. Even when their content is irrelevant or ill-adapted to the lives of the people who study them these favoured subjects remain pre-eminent in the eyes of students, parents, teachers and employers, while other subjects in the formal curriculum tend to be associated with inferior ability and poorer prospects. Environmental education as a fringe activity, however exciting, can be seen as less serious, more recreational. When pressures mount, such as examination diets or financial constraints, they are more easily dropped. To achieve for environmental education the status which we desire, this citadel of educational orthodoxy must be breached.

Appropriate strategies may be 'top-down' and 'bottom-up', probably both if possible. Success in either direction depends on having a clear idea in practical terms of what one wishes to do. What follows is a review of the things which make education of any kind environmental. It is largely built round a 'bottom-up' approach which was pioneered with some success in the west of Scotland and which is later summarised as a case study.

WHERE HAS EDUCATION GONE WRONG?

Education is defined by the Oxford English Dictionary as the process of preparing people for the work of life. Since this work can only be performed in an environment of some sort it is reasonable to inquire why education should ever need to be distinguished as 'environmental'.

For most of our fellow creatures success in life is a matter of doing what they are programmed to do, in whatever timespan good fortune allows them, and as part of the environmental system in which their kind has evolved. For us it is more difficult. Our physical and mental capacities which allow us to remember, to foresee, to communicate complex messages across space and time, to imagine and to create, partially free us from the constraints of our physical inheritance and our surroundings. Cultural systems, that we can control, change far more rapidly and extensively than the biological systems which they overlie, and have overturned our relationship with our world. But not wholly: the biological systems remain, and the tensions set up through maladjustments of the cultural to the biological systems break out in all sorts of undesirable forms, affecting us in ways ranging from personal health and behaviour to global conflict. And the freedom in any case is only conditional. If by our free will we cannot better regulate our relationships with our world it is entirely possible that our world may dispense with us. It is therefore becoming a matter of survival that we now focus our capacities, skills and understanding on the adjustment of human behaviour to a pattern that will enable us to continue as part of the global system, to learn for ourselves what our fellow creatures do not require to learn.

Education has always been part of the process by which people became fitted to live successfully in their world. At one time, in our remote past, it must have been a matter of acquiring physical skills and developing the stamina to use them, of discovering how to gather from one's surroundings the variety of resources needed to maintain healthy life, and of learning from one's elders and one's peers the obligations and constraints on behaviour necessary to live as a member of a social group, whether family or tribe. At that stage all education was environmental.

The recent history of the human species has, however, been marked by technological and social changes which have vastly extended its capacity to exploit natural resources, to reorganise them in ways to suit itself and to enjoy thereby the fruits of wealth and leisure, or at least hope to enjoy them. Naturally, education grew to reflect this by preparing people to employ the scientific and technical resources of their expanding world, to apprehend the more complex philosophical and social systems that succeeded tribal wisdom and to enjoy the cultural and recreational activities made possible by leisure time. The environment which sustained these changes became relegated to the stage on which humankind performs and a seemingly limitless source of materials and power to be commanded at will.

Now, as we see more clearly the limits of the earth's capacity to meet our demands, it has become plain that our education must change again in its recognition of the environment. On the one hand, we must recover our ancient capacity to see ourselves as part of our world, the two being interdependent; at the same time we must redirect our technological and social development towards harmony and sustainability rather than exploitation and indulgence. This is what makes environmental education different and it amounts to a revision of our whole educational philosophy.

THE MAN-ENVIRONMENT SYSTEM

The cornerstone of environmental education is the identification of individual with environment, as inseparable and interdependent parts of a single entity. To be a part of our environment is to be alive, to be separated from it can only mean death. It starts with the elements of air and earth and water with which we are immediately in contact all the time, and extends outwards through people and places to spheres unfelt and unseen but still not unconnected. It is always in a state of change, dynamic, with a history that helps to explain its present state and point towards its future. We depend on it always and in all sorts of ways, some short term and some long term, so the changes affect us and we affect them. Some at least are under our control. The health of our environmnent is part of our own health: to be healthy we must care for both, so we try to direct change in the way that is best for the whole system.

It follows that, to be environmental, education will always identify, explore and take into account as far as possible the variety of components of the system. The easiest starting point is generally those things which connect directly to ourselves - the system to which we belong most closely. Early in life these things are few and fairly simple but as education progresses the connections multiply and extend further and further out, from home to more distant places, from family to less familiar people, from the present to stories of the past and hopes for the future. We learn by everyday experience how many of the components interact but environmental education should help us discover many more, to 'look round the backs of things', to find out how one thing affects another. The better we learn the better should be our repertoire of behaviour towards our environment. Education moves most effectively from the familiar to the unfamiliar expanding the system with which we identify, and from the concrete to the abstract providing concepts which we can use to interpret the growing complexities of the system. How well we are educated will be partly a function of the quality and richness of the environment in which we develop. Educators seek to enhance these influences.

Many of the things which most affect our behavioural development, especially in early life, are not usually thought of as education, even non-formal. They are the physical, social and cultural characteristics of the world in which we grow up, provided by other people to their own standards for their own purposes, without consideration for any effects they may have on the developing young. As we now know their influence extends forwards even into prenatal life through the maternal environment. Environmental education is concerned with the quality of the human environment for healthy development as well as for healthy life.

Since we are promoting a systems approach to the study of our environment it is only fair to the man-environment entity that we adopt a systems approach to its human centre. How a person behaves is a product of internal as well as external factors. This is the environmnent of physiological needs, real or imagined, the capacities of the body to perform as required, the limitations on perception imposed by sensory systems, the modifying effects of past experience, attitudes to the behaviour and communications of others, emotional states, imaginative and creative capacities and so on.

This makes the man-environment interaction more complex than first appears: one can distinguish between:

(i)   The theoretical total environment, to much of which we are not directly connected and with little direct effect on us, although it may be important through secondary or higher order connections with other components of our system;

(ii)   The immediate environment, those components of (i) with which we are in direct contact although we may remain unaware of them even with the help of instrumentation;

(iii)   The potential perceptual environment, consisting of all the things which we could perceive (but many of which we may nevertheless ignore or be untrained to detect);

(iv)   The realised perceptual environment which is what we think we are aware of (after filtration, interpretation in the light of other experience and the intervention of unrecognised obstructions).

Because of this our effective environment is bound to be an individual one even when compared with that of the people we live with, and of course widely different from that of fellow creatures. For an understanding of it we are as much dependent on the arts as on the sciences since they take account of many things beyond the reach of measurement. Our responses to our perceived environment are also likely to be structured in a similar way. Environmental education should therefore aim to improve the quality of the realised perceptual environment, develop understanding of the influences which restrict or modify it, by raising the quality of information improve the capacity for acting responsibly within it, and, by heightening aesthetic awareness, improve sensitivity to its less tangible qualities and develop creative responsiveness.

SOME IDEAS TO DISCOURAGE

The idea of 'the environment' as something 'out there' rather than here and now lingers still in educational usage. Some traditional biology syllabuses, for example, still segregate ecology into a separate section (often at the end, to be conducted in summer weather if at all) and direct studies towards 'well defined habitats'. Even more up-to-date schemes of work in social or modern studies treat 'the environment' as a separate field of interest (the habitat of 'environmentalists'?). These treatments are reflected by public and media in, for example, the identification of 'green' parties and conservation lobbies as distinct from, and perhaps in competition with, other parties and lobbies more obviously identified with power and prosperity. Designated studies of ecology, environmental planning, environmental health and so on have their important places in education but the environment as a component of any and every human activity cannot be isolated: perhaps we have to work hard to restore the true definition of the word before it becomes irretrievably misunderstood.

Another surviving tendency is to separate mankind and his works, in everyday usage, from a so-called natural environment as if he were unnatural. Plainly this is not so: for all his special capacities he is not biologically so distinct. Similarly urban and rural are set apart as if the middle-ground between them scarcely exists. The environmental educator must be wary of slick classification that may obscure understanding.

There is a pervasive idea that environmental education is mainly concerned with problems. Problems are there, of course, in plenty and most of them very complex. Because they are well publicised and often expensive they can provide ready arguments for use in persuading those in authority to support environmental education (which should be a means of creating a better informed citizenry perhaps supportive of measures to allay the problems). Likewise the problems, because of relevance of topicality, offer tempting topics on which to base classroom teaching. How often, for example, do we find 'pollution' as a lead topic? (In some environmentally concerned schools it has led to senior pupils saying 'not again!' to yet another exposure to the problem - a counter-productive exposure if ever there was one). The problem having been stated, how is it then to be solved? Many of these are mega-problems which are still taxing the wisdom of experts: the complexities of the systems from which such problems emerge are generally well beyond the reach of school science, let alone their links to economics, politics and other disciplines. The result in the classroom is apt to be dismissed by experts in the field as over-simplification, misrepresentation, ill-judged analyses, naive solutions, the kinds of things, in short, which environmental education is supposed to guide people to avoid. This does not help to promote support for environmental education.

Does this mean that environmental educators should not touch such important and topical issues as acid deposition, nuclear residues and pesticide contamination? Certainly not: but the pretence of solving the problem is not necessary. It is important to see problems in their context, to explore the interacting components of the systems in which they occur, the human influence on their development, the conflicting value judgements that affect choices of action and the options open to those who can eventually act. There are good case-studies available and they should be studied, but critically. Problems of this sort are in a sense diseases of the system. For the layman it may be more a case of formulating problems than solving them. There is a special need to look for the prophylactic measures needed to prevent recurrence. Detailed research is for the specialist and its interpretation for consultants who can well be brought in to advise.

Furthermore, important as they are, problems are a poor way of presenting normality. The positive approach is through health not disease, beauty not blemishes. If young people have first learned to appreciate and care for their world and the provisions that it makes for their happiness, then they will come to view its ailments with a proper concern for their treatment. The skills of problem-solving are important, but most valuable if the student is first motivated and able to see what is wrong.

In a rather similar category is the idea of the 'environmental crisis'. The case for environmental education is often presented as a response to a crisis. But a crisis, according to the Oxford English Dictionary is 'a vitally important or decisive stage in the progress of anything; a turning-point; also a state of affairs in which a decisive change for better or worse is imminent'. Most of the changes in the man-environment system, which have led to such documents as the World Conservation Strategy (IUCN 1980), do not quite fit that. Mostly they have been relatively slow, insidious and unseen. Although many have now become evident there is no particular sign of a turning-point one way or the other, just steady continuation or acceleration; or, if we make large and determined efforts, perhaps deceleration and then reversal. To see on television the haunting consequences of Sahelian desertification does not mean that a crisis-point has been reached, and it could be dangerously misleading to suppose that might be so. It is important, therefore, for environmental education to represent fairly the timescale of change. The OED adds to the quotation above 'now applied esp. to times of difficulty, insecurity and suspense': perhaps we should settle for that.

IDENTIFYING PRINCIPLES

By way of summary we can now state on the evidence of need that education, to be environmental, should subscribe to the following:

(i)   Basic Concepts

-    It is founded on the inseparability of human subject and environment;

-    It recognises environment as encompassing physical, spatial, social and temporal components, along with their aesthetic, cultural, political and economic characteristics;

-    It emphasises the interconnectedness of things through interlocking systems of increasing magnitude from the individual to the biosphere;

-    It recognises the enabling and constraining properties of energy and material resources;

-    It recognises the uniqueness of the individual and selectivity to input and output;

-    It recognises the corresponding uniqueness of individual environments;

-    It recognises the effects of human lifestyles on short-term and long-term change, their causes and costs.

(ii)   Approaches

-    It draws on the expertise of virtually all subject disciplines;

-    It aims to achieve holistic perspectives;

-    It is rooted in the immediate personal environment of the individual and his or her behaviour towards it;

-    It aims to provide progressive enrichment of

environmental experience, balanced between the different aspects of the environment;

- Although it starts from the familiar it extends globally in recognition of the ultimate unity of the biosphere;

- It seeks to integrate the external and internal environments of the individual;

- It recognises that development, including learning, is much affected by the environment in which it happens;

- It is problem-formulating rather than problem-solving and emphasises the need for co-operation with both specialists and those with local knowledge;

- It operates in open rather than in closed situations and aims to be anticipatory rather than corrective;

- It favours systematic rather than linear thinking;

- It combines cognitive with affective learning;

- It recognises the complementarity of art and science in environmental learning;

- It lays value on such characteristics as quality, diversity, sustainability, flexibility, efficiency, co-operation, balance, long-term benefit, equitability.

(iii)   Skills

- It develops sensory capacities;

- It enhances data-acquisition by use of instrumentation;

- It uses a variety of secondary sources including oral and archive sources;

- It develops skills of measurement and of assessment;

- It utilises a variety of forms of codification, compilation, presentation and communication of data;

- It gives practice in formulating and testing hypotheses;

- It develops skills of prediction and evaluation;

- It develops interpretative and creative skills;

- It develops skills of constructive participation with others.

(iv)   Attitudes

- It develops a caring attitude and a sense of responsibility for the well-being of the system;

- It encourages a critical attitude to received information, a questioning of assumptions, and caution as to the reliability of personal interpretation;

- It promotes a sense of identity and continuity with the environment and respect for its structures and processes;

- It extends the sense of community with other people and other living things;

- It encourages a sense of continuity with past and future;

- It promotes respect for the unique human capacity to overcome biological and other environmental constraints and to design the future creatively;

- It develops a commitment to contribute personal talents to participation in improving environmental quality.

Such a programme will be life-long and should permeate all of education in the widest sense; it is unconfined by institutions and not dependent on any particular kind of environment although it will be favoured by diversity of experience. Underlying it there is an ethical foundation which incorporates the environment into the human systems of belief. This is an area of very active development at present and all that there is space to do here is to acknowledge its importance and to suggest that its main precepts are as likely to emerge from the ecological realities of the man-environment system as from anywhere.

The organisation of environmental education can now be divided between the treatment appropriate to particular topics and the approaches to designing a comprehensive scheme of education.

AN ENVIRONMENTAL APPROACH TO TOPICS

For reasons that have already been suggested, environmental learning comes most readily through specific topics, whether they are units of an environmental course or within the syllabus of a specific subject discipline. There are several advantages of this approach. For example:

(i) Mention has already been made of basing environmental teaching on things which are familiar and issues which are topical and not too abstract. There are sound and familiar educational reasons for this, and in the modern world even exotic topics and faraway places have direct connections to known starting points.

(ii) The unit of environmental experience and of human behaviour is always the individual in his own environment. This is the first level at which to look for cause as a means of understanding consequence and the first level at which to seek the cure for an environmental problem. If one knows about individuals and how they respond to specific issues, one can move to progressively larger social systems with more certainty and a better chance of understanding.

(iii) The complexities of real systems can be better appreciated by reference to a familiar issue, and the difficulties of relating causes and consequences, with all their contributory influences, more easily understood.

(iv) It is a better means of developing the desired sense of personal responsibility for environmental quality, rather than devolving it on an impersonal 'they' who should 'do something'.

To see one way in which a topic may be treated to give the possibility of a balance environmental approach, we now turn to a model devised by a group in the west of Scotland.

THE STRATHCLYDE MODEL

The first step in organising or renovating a programme of education is to gather together a group of people representing the range of interests and experience that it represents. Having established such a group the next stage is to ask them to say specifically why they feel their task is necessary and what they want to do. Inevitably this leads to rather theoretical discussion, and the re-exploration of some quite well-trodden ground. But it is necessary if only to encourage fresh thinking and ensure that the special features of the educational environment in which they are working are incorporated in the design of what they hope to do. They will clearly have to concern themselves with:

the aims and contents of their programme (epistemological factors);

the physical, social, political and cultural context in which it is presented (environmental factors);

the age and experience of those to whom it is directed (developmental factors).

In doing this they will be reminded that they are working with a bipartite system in which people and environment are inseparately integrated. They will also find their way afresh to well-established characteristics of the programme they need to promote and the reasons why it is necessary.

The Strathclyde Environmental Education Group was a quite informal gathering of practitioners of this sort which set itself the task of developing ideas current in Scotland in the mid-seventies and adapting them for work in school. It roughly followed the above line of approach. Accounts of the group and its work are to be found in papers by Forbes and Smyth (1984) and Crawford (1985) and their teaching model has been published by the Scottish Curriculum Development Service (Strathclyde EE Group, 1984).

The Group was originally concerned with the 14 to 16 age group. Their model, which they tested successfully in schools, could easily be adapted, however, to any level of education and to informal as well as formal education.

Following its initial discussions of the nature and scope of environmental education, the group produced a definition of its aims as follows:

> The aim of Environmental Education is to enable people to recognise the factors which determine the nature and quality of the human environment so that all may respect and appreciate it to the full and participate constructively, as individuals and as citizens, in its management and development.

This was followed by a set of objectives:

> To identify, and observe more accurately the many components to our environmnent;

> To understand the inter-relationships and inter-dependence between these components and ourselves;

> To evaluate the aims and environmental consequences of our activities;

> To act, directly and indirectly, in a manner which will ensure the maintenance of a harmonious relationship between man and the world in which he lives.

These were reformed as a set of five key questions, adapted to suit the subject matter, but basically as follows:

> What does it look like (sound, taste, feel etc)?

> How does it come to be like that?

> How do the bits fit together, and how does it work?

> How does it change?

> How is this change controlled?

By this means they aimed to develop:

> environmental awareness by quantitative study;

> the ability to recognise and to understand inter-relationships;

an aesthetic awareness to include recognition of human influence and encourage respect for the perceptions of other people;

a sense of responsibility for the environment and of a need for personal participation in its management;

the appropriate skills of observation, measurement, recording, communication, evaluation and collaborative action in the guidance of change.

For its trial run, the topic chosen was housing. The team managing the project produced a set of course objectives by breaking down each of the key questions into appropriate elements. These objectives could be further classified as knowledge, comprehension, higher abilities, communication, practical and attitudinal, and geared to student age and abilities. More specific objectives were then put together by each of the participating schools to suit its own local circumstances. The schools were also provided with checklists for introductory components of the course (e.g. contextual statements), curricular components (e.g. suggestions for learning activities), resource lists and sources of support, and assessment procedures such as student self-checks.

The model proved successful in the opinions of both teachers and students. The following quotations from school reports at the end of the project are representative:

the best recommendation for the model under test is that it is planned to continue using it as a basis for our course. It is a simple, logical and easy to understand guide to the planning of a course which allows teachers from different subject areas to see exactly where they can contribute most effectively, also the model is equally useful for any topic within the course, as our preliminary planning has shown to us.

The Environmental Topic is the best thing in our course. Children welcome the change in pace. The opportunities for learning in a less formal setting are huge.

Fuller accounts of the model can be found in the

references already quoted. It was prepared as a guide to the environmental treatment of a familiar topic and taught as part of non-examinable environmental courses in the trial schools, using teaching teams drawn from several relevant subject areas. While a full-scale, topic-based, inter-disciplinary environmental course, to be followed by all children through their school career, might be an ideal prescription, it is not likely to be realised, in this country at least, unless education receives a major reorganisation. The reasons for this include the inflexibility of administrative systems, the strength of established subject disciplines and the low rating given, by pupils, parents and teachers alike, to any subject which does not contribute materially to success in qualifying examinations and entry to higher education or employment. If every student, including the most able, is to be educated environmentally, at least beyond the age of 11 or so, then an environmental approach must be adopted to subjects of established status already within the curriculum. Since a multi-disciplinary teaching team is unlikely in these circumstances the principle of using other teachers or outside experts as visiting consultants is one which must be encouraged, a practice which has the additional advantage of mirroring what happens in real life when a multi-faceted problem has to be analysed.

In Scotland a step in this direction was taken when one of the original team became involved in the drafting of a new secondary science syllabus and was instrumental in introducing the principles of the Strathclyde model to relevant parts of it. In the light of his experience he contributed a valuable case study on influencing curriculum development to the Bangalore conference on 'Science and Technology Education and Future Human Needs' (Crawford 1985), which will also appear in a shortened version in Baez et al. (1987). Further experiments with the model in Scottish schools have been inhibited by a variety of recent upheavals in the system but the group hopes that its influence will continue to be felt.

In summary, the Strathclyde model offers a guide to treating a great variety of topics in an environmental manner, whether they are individual topics, parts of an environmental course or parts of other courses. It is adaptable to levels of education other than secondary and to informal as well as formal education. It does not pretend, however, to be a full answer to the question posed in the title. It is also necessary to consider larger structures.

THE QUESTION OF CONTENT

Topics are necessarily limited units of teaching and individually will only go a small way towards the objectives of environmental education. Whether one is dealing with an extended integrated programme or with selected topics distributed through other subjects there is a need to arrange one's choices of subject matter in a way that will be reinforcing, not haphazard. This raises the question of course content.

Content is apt to give trouble to course designers who wish to emphasise approaches, methods of investigation, values and attitudes rather than factual recall. Obviously, knowledge of certain things is necessary, as a basis for the development of concepts, acquisition of skills and fostering of attitudes. If it is written down as a syllabus, however, and used to supply the criteria for testing, it is all too apt to become the main end of teaching while the more important objectives are neglected. Fortunately much of the necessary knowledge may already be in the school curriculum, scattered among many relevant subjects. If so the objectives of the environmental educator should be capable of protection by effective co-ordination, cross-reference and inter-subject collaboration. An 'in-school' co-ordination system - whether by an individual or a committee - is therefore important.

The detailed knowledge needed for environmental study is as diverse as the schools and the localities in which they work. More general accounts of environmental systems and how to manage them fill many shelves and are increasing daily, as indeed are teaching materials and methodologies relating to them. The problem here is to identify and select relevant material, and then to adapt it to specific local conditions, a task for which practising teachers have little time and need much more help. The concepts which have to be drawn out somewhere in an environmental education scheme are fortunately less diverse.

As a guide to selection all young people should be introduced to a range of experiences from which the objectives of an environmental course may be expected to be accessible and these can be stated in fairly general terms adaptable to local circumstances. The five key areas of the Strathclyde model offer a convenient structure (bearing in mind that a list is an artificial and confusing way of representing a web of interconnections):

(i)   <u>Observation</u> covers a range of things including:

People and the things they do, extending from ourselves and our families outwards to people of other countries with whom we may be linked but whom we may never see:

life from conception to death;

needs - air, food, water, fuels, shelter, companionship, status etc;

work and leisure activities, and transport between them;

health and a sense of well-being;

differentials in consumption patterns;

special knowledge and skills;

ideas of quality of life, and aspirations for the future;

cultural diversity;

population growth and resources.

Places where their activities take place:

home, school, neighbourhood;

work, service and recreation areas;

holiday areas;

villages, towns, cities, cultivated and uncultivated countryside;

coast and sea;

connections to more distant places at home or abroad.

Characteristics of the places:

climate and weather;

topography, geology, soil, minerals;

water;

vegetation, animals, micro-organisms;

building styles, functions and densities;

transport and communication systems.

(ii) Evidence of change and how things have come to be as they are:

family history;

local history, including oral history and local records;

cultural history, including folklore and the arts;

technological history;

population movement;

land use history, including agriculture, forestry, water and energy;

natural history, including changing flora and fauna;

climatic and geological history;

projections of future history.

(iii) Interconnections and functions, involving the assembly of simple systems, analysis of familiar patterns, recognition of the determinants of systems, constraints and limitations on processes of change:

Natural connections:

energy flows, including energy storage and energy dissipation;

cycling of materials, including biodegradation;

information flow, including genetic information, and

human and non-human communication;

co-evolution and co-adaptation;

maintenance of balance and recovery from perturbation.

Man-induced change:

physical alteration of land by cultivation, building, extraction etc;

exploitation of renewable and non-renewable resources;

alteration and re-distribution of plants and animals, including creation of pests and spread of diseases;

movement of resources between country and town and around the world;

disposal of wastes of land, sea and air;

distortions of energy flow and inequitable resource consumption;

birth and mortality control;

warfare and its environmental implications.

(iv) Evaluating courses of change relating the evidence of changing states to the processes which govern them and predicting how to optimise benefit for both man and environment; comparing also one's own with community needs and aspirations:

Recognition of ecological values such as:

long-term predictability or stability and capacity for recovery from perturbation;

diversity (especially important in a modern world where imposed conformity in behaviour and repetitive monotony in building are often the rule);

information content including the conservation of

genetic resources;

sustainability in the context of human use of resources.

Recognition of societal values including:

structural and design qualities, safety, efficiency, comfort;

cost-benefit relationships;

aesthetic values;

ideas of freedom of action, of rights and of duties;

cultural values, including religious and ethical values;

fair distribution of resources, including recognition of special needs, e.g. of the unborn, the very young, the old, the handicapped, the socially disadvantaged.

Recognition of different means of assessment, e.g.:

economic criteria;

energy criteria (see, for example, the work of Odum and Odum 1981);

aesthetic criteria;

ethical criteria (stemming from the developing concepts of environmental ethics).

(v) The guidance of change, recognising that environmental education without the prospect of action to remedy deficiencies is unconvincing, and that the capacity for creative management and guidance of change is the special gift of humankind:

forecasting futures for the unplanned system;

designing alternative futures;

legislation and the role of local and national government agencies;

influence of political bodies;

planning procedures;

the role of non-governmental agencies;

the role of international agencies;

resource-use management;

conservation of the natural heritage, landscape, biosphere resources;

conservation of the cultural heritage;

conservation of the human species, sound in body and mind.

Given something like the above list the curriculum planner will readily understand that in its totality it is impossible and that he must select from it. Whether he is looking at the entire school career from nursery to university entrance, or only at the assembly of a short course within a single year of study, his planning will have to include:

the time available to him and its distribution within the week and within the year;

the resources available in staff, space, facilities and materials, travel and outside assistance;

the numbers, ages, ability levels and experience of the target groups;

the physical, social and cultural environment of the school itself.

It was envisaged by the Strathclyde group that its model would be part of a spiral process of course development, with a movement in emphasis from the simpler skills of observation, measurement and recording, towards more complex understanding in system relationships and eventually to the higher abilities called for by evaluation and action. Nevertheless, all of the key questions have a role of some sort at every stage of education. Nursery school children hold some very definite views about environment management.

PUTTING A SCHEME TOGETHER

We now have several sets of criteria which can be used to determine if a course truly meets the description 'environmental' as we have defined it. A set of topics is drawn up, whether as a separate programme or as a set contained within existing subject of the curriculum and abstracted for the purpose of assessment. The set can then be combined with each of several sets of criteria to provide matrices by which the course can be judged overall. The sets of criteria would include:

- a set of objectives of environmental education, comprising knowledge and concepts, skills and attitudes (e.g. as suggested earlier, or simplified);

- a set of issues, such as that above, or an appropriate modification of it;

- a set of stages in the school career, if the programme extends over such a period;

- a set of contributory subject disciplines, if the programme is to be met in this way;

- a set of teaching methods to ensure maximum variety of activity and learning experience;

- a set of outside agencies which might be required to aid with resources or advice.

More are possible. There will never be a set of topics which is a perfect fit for all of these criteria, but the exercise will show up the gaps and if they are serious the topic list can be revised. A readiness for sensible compromise is one of the personal qualities which the environmentalist has to accept.

LAST POINTS

It has always been emhasised that the Strathclyde model is

adaptable to other sectors of education as a means of adopting the environmental approach. Some consideration has recently been given to it in adult education, for example. It also offers a structuring system to informal educators whose role is of great importance for the achievement of the stated objectives.

There is much evidence that the behaviour of people towards their environment is greatly influenced not only by what they know about it but by their past experience of it. Pleasurable experience of the countryside, for example, is an important dominant of support for conservation and may also determine what it is the subject mostly wishes to conserve (not necessarily what the conservation lobbies support). School can and should play an important part in supplying this experience, through expeditions, camps, field courses and so on.

Whatever the school supplies, life out of school may override it. Environmental educators have a duty to work for a public environment (and indeed for a school environment) which conforms more closely to the standards they promote. And reform starts close to home: educators who are not seen to rule their own lives by the values they profess, or conduct their teaching in the conditions they advocate, may well be lost.

The 'top-down' approach to educational reform is needed as well as the 'bottom-up'. What support do we require of those who determine the overall structure of education and those who administer it in schools?

-   In universities, professional institutions and employers' organisations a commitment to environmental competence as one of the qualities needed for progress in learning and employment - reflected in the qualifications they set for entry to their respective institutions;

-   In those bodies that construct and control school curricula, including examination boards, a recognition of the need both to modify and to co-ordinate environmental teaching through the school career;

-   In school administrations an acceptance of the need for support and a degree of flexibility in timetabling and staffing, and the appointment of a co-ordinator or co-ordinating committee within the school;

- In teacher training colleges a commitment to training in environmental approaches and methods for all teachers, including experience of out-of-school work and the use of external consultants and resources.

Do we want a revolution in education to achieve our objectives completely? Probably not: we can learn from ecology that a major perturbation opens the field to opportunists with short term objectives and a lot of energy to expend in competition. Under the stress of a major upheaval the survivors of an educational revolution would most probably be the interests with the most power and the simplest rewards, and environmental education does not fit that description. So it is perhaps less risky to concentrate on adapting and adjusting existing structures, albeit as quickly as we can. But the process must be genuine and comprehensive, carried out with conviction, in circumstances which conform as far as possible with the standards of quality that environmental education commends.

BIBLIOGRAPHY

Baez, A.V., Knamiller, G. & Smyth, J.C. (eds.) 1987. The Environment and Science and Technology Education. Pergamon Press, Oxford.

Crawford, F., 1985. Environmental education courses in Scotland: a case study of theory translated into practice. Science and Technology and Future Human Needs, Bangalore: ICSU, Paris.

Forbes, J. and Smyth, J.C., 1984. 'Structuring environmental education - a Strathclyde model'. The Environmentalist, 4(3), 196-204.

IUCN (International Union for the Conservation of Nature and Natural Resources) 1980. World Conservation Strategy, Gland, Switzerland.

Odum, H.T. & Odum, E.C., 1981. Energy Basis for Man and Nature, McGraw Hill, New York.

Strathclyde Environmental Education Group, 1984. The Environment, a Learning Experience, Scottish Curriculum Development Service, Jordanhill College of Education, Glasgow.

Chapter Three

THE EDUCATIONAL SIDE OF ENVIRONMENTAL EDUCATION[1]

Kerst Th. Boersma

INTRODUCTION

Discussions about environmental education (EE) tend to concentrate more often on its desired content and less often on how it should be organised in order to secure the desired effect. Too much is said, in my view, about the environmental side of the subject and too little about the educational side, and certainly too little about the models, theories and research findings on which the educational side can be based. In other words, many of the objectives set for EE relate too much to what is regarded as desirable and too little to the reality of educational science.

In this article I shall be putting the emphasis on the educational side of EE. In doing so I shall be associating myself with the description of education contained in the new basic philosophy put forward by the (Dutch) State Advisory Committee on Environmental Education (CNBE 1985). In that document, education is taken to mean learning situations directed towards the achievement of concrete instructional objectives within a predetermined period of time, situations which are built up logically and in a structured manner and involving a specifically described group of participants.

I shall put forward theories, models and research findings, drawn from educational science, teaching methodology and pedagogy, which in my opinion can help to amplify the educational side of EE. Before doing so I would make the following marginal comments:

- Firstly, I shall be dealing particularly with EE in schools. This is the area I am most familiar with and I would maintain provisionally that much of what can be proposed with regard to EE in schools is also applicable to EE in other settings.

- Secondly, what I have to say is not the full story; many important aspects will be dealt with not at all or only in passing.

- Thirdly, the theories, models and research of educational science, psychology, teaching methodology and pedagogy are subject to change. A great deal is still being debated, including the underlying assumptions.

I shall start by examining some problems of objectives of EE (not the objectives), discussing both the nature and the content of objectives. I shall then examine the organisation of the subject matter of EE: in what order must or may subjects, which are regarded as important for EE, be offered.

OBJECTIVES, AIMS AND GOALS OF EE

To give an impression of the nature of objectives, aims and goals, I shall first quote some examples, including some from recent Dutch publications.

> Environmental education is the process of recognising values and clarifying concepts in order to develop skills and attitudes necessary to understand and appreciate the inter-relatedness of man, his culture and his biophysical surroundings...
> Environmental education also entails practice in decision-making and self-formulation of a code of behaviour about issues concerning environmental quality.
>
> (IUCN, Nevada Conference, 1970)
>
> Environmental education is the development of a process of becoming aware of the natural environment, an environment which is influenced by man. This development, which stems from learning through discovery (for onself), must be directed towards furthering a pattern of responsible behaviour in relation to man's surroundings as a totality and towards developing skills which promote participation in opinion-forming and decision-making processes in the sphere of the environment.

The goal of environmental education is to improve pupils' ecological awareness and hence their environmental behaviour, and also to put them in a position to adopt attitudes or hold opinions on social developments.

The ultimate aim of environmental education is: on the basis of experience of and insight into the coexistence of humans, plants, animals and inanimate objects, to become aware of each person's responsibility towards the environment and to participate creatively in that environment.

It is immediately noticeable, without any need to analyse these objectives in detail, that:

- the objectives relate to acquisition of knowledge, insight, awareness, skills, attitudes and values and to affecting changes in patterns of behaviour,

- the objectives are directed towards individual self-realisation and/or towards changing the structure of society.

I will examine both points in greater detail.

The Nature of Objectives, Aims and Goals of EE

It is no exaggeration to say that man's continued existence is seriously threatened by the way he has thus far treated his environment and its natural resources. It was not for nothing that the World Conservation Strategy (WCS) was set up (IUCN 1980).

Some people hold that any means of changing human behaviour is permissible if it averts this threat; but to adopt this approach would be to open the door to every kind of indoctrination. The pedagogical literature, and this also applies in my opinion to the majority of people today, is virtually unanimous in believing that teaching must not consist of mindless drills or covert attempts to influence thinking and behaviour. Indoctrination has thus been rejected.

Is effective EE possible, then?

There seems to be a paradox here. If you do not influence learners in the desired direction, you contribute to allowing our society to remain unchanged - with a possibility

59

of total destruction; but if you do influence learners in the desired direction, you contribute to bringing into existence an undesirable form of society, which may itself possibly lead to a great deal of misery.

I cannot solve this paradox; I can, however, show that there is only one option, not two. I do so on the basis of two theoretical points of reference.

1. Watzlawick has formulated a communication theory about the way in which people influence each other (Watzlawick and others, 1967). This theory states emphatically that people cannot help influencing each other, so you exert influence all the time, whether intentionally or not.[2]

   Another point that Watzlawick has shown is that the result of attempts to evoke specific feelings or attitudes can never be predicted; indeed if the learner has no other option open to him, such attempts can lead to paradoxical situations. You cannot force people to have specific feelings, to find specific things important or, for example, to care for the environment.

2. Standards and values are based on meanings which people attribute to things. Meanings which young people have learned to attribute to things, in particular, persist stubbornly. The 'attributable theory' refers specifically to this.

   This theory states that the meaning which the learner will attribute to things is determined principally by the ideas he already has about them, and that, if he is confronted with conflicting ideas, his learning may be blocked. This leads to 'cognitive dissonance' (Festinger, 1957).

The above theories state on the one hand that it is impossible not to influence pupils and on the other that it is impossible deliberately to make pupils learn things which are based on meanings which they must attribute to things (specific attitudes, standards and values).

To escape this threatening paradox, the following description of an instructional objective - taken from De Groot, a well-known Dutch educational theorist - might be useful.

An instructional objective is a result which is regarded as desirable, a result which has the character of a mental programme which is to be acquired deliberately by the pupil and which must be added to and/or incorporated in what he has already learned so far.

(De Groot, 1978)

Therefore specific values, standards and attitudes have no place in instructional objectives. EE objectives should entail the planned realisation of desired results. EE objectives must thus focus on extending the pupil's behavioural repertoire, on things which he may do if he wishes to, and on extending mental programmes, the cognitive structure on which a pupil may base specific behaviour if he wishes to do so.

To prevent misunderstandings, the following should be noted: Firstly, you can distinguish between aims or goals on the one hand and objectives on the other. Aims or goals are something you might have at the back of your mind which act as a sort of continuous guiding thread for you but which do not form the concrete basis for your teaching. Objectives are the specific ideas on which the content of your teaching is based.

Secondly, this is not - of course - to say that EE should not or could not contribute to the development of standards, values and attitudes on the environment, but that specific standards, values and attitudes cannot be taught according to a deliberate plan. Mental programmes which are to be deliberately acquired can, however, be so taught. Learners can indeed develop standards, values and attitudes on the environnment on the basis of the meanings which they already attribute to elements of it. An EE teaching methodology which is directed towards this end, partly on the basis of actively coming into contact with elements in the environment, is certainly possible and could be very important for pupils' individual development.

The Content of EE Objectives

In connection with the objectives of EE, there is often advocacy, to a greater or lesser extent, for individual self-realisation or for the interests of society. To put it more specifically; should EE be geared to the individual's experience of nature or to changing the structures of society that cause and maintain environmental problems?

This apparent opposition of two alternatives is illusory. To explain this, another theoretical choice can be made, a very obvious choice when it is a matter of ecological content. Von Bertalanffy's general system theory (Von Bertalanffy, 1968), and especially the idea that different organisational levels can be distinguished, is very important for the formulation of objectives for EE. This is obviously not so strange in view of the fact that since Odum 'system ecology' has occupied an important position within ecology as a whole.

The starting point for the formulation of EE objectives must be the idea that people are part of systems, both individually and collectively. These systems may include each other, in that one system may simultaneously consist of elements which can in turn be regarded as systems, being themselves elements in a higher ranking system. Every individual, whether he wants to or not, is thus part of systems of different hierarchical levels. Most Dutch people are individual elements in the following hierarchical series of systems:

(a)   family and immediate surroundings (home)

(b)   neighbourhood

(c)   municipality

(d)   the Netherlands

(e)   the European Community

(f)   the biosphere/the world

Within these systems everyone has influence on the other elements of the system and contributes - consciously or unconsciously - to maintaining the system in existence. In some of these systems the influence is greater, in others less. Man's influence - especially collectively - is often so great that he does not realise that he too is influenced by the non-human elements of the system and is dependent on such elements for his continued existence. It is important that the exerting of influence between each individual and the other elements in the systems in which each individual is a part should find expression in EE objectives. This is supported by the following arguments:

- realising that you have influence contributes to the attainment of an important pedagogical goal: strengthening the sense of identity.

- realising that you have influence enables you to act more in accordance with your intentions.

- realising that the continued existence of the systems you belong to depends on the way in which influence is exerted between yourself and the other elements removes the conflict between individual self-realisation and the interests of society.

Two possible EE objectives could therefore be:

- teaching people to see how they have an influence on the elements of the systems of which they are part and how they themselves are influenced by the other elements (human, biotic and abiotic).

- teaching pupils to see how (i.e. by what behaviour) they can use their influence within the systems of which they are part, bearing in mind the desired effects on the other elements of those systems and the need for the continued existence of those systems as such.

The advantages of these objectives are:

1. The conflict between individual and social aspects is removed from the objectives.

2. The objectives lend themselves well to being further elaborated - by system, by nature of influence and also by nature of the elements.

3. The objectives meet the conditions formulated in 2.1: they are directed towards extension of the repertoire of behaviour and extension of knowledge and insight on the basis of which behaviour choices can be made.

4. The objectives make no distinction between natural and non-natural systems. The objectives relate to the whole material world, i.e. they also cover those social systems

in which the elements (people or groups of people) belong to the material world).[3]

Recommendations

In 'The Nature of Objectives, Aims and Goals of EE', 2.1, we advocated objectives which can be elaborated into learning results realisable in a planned way. In 'The Content of EE Objectives' we put forward a framework, namely system theory, 2.2, with the aid of which objectives can be formulated which not only fulfil this purpose but also have other advantages.

To give a rather more specific direction to EE, the following two proposals are made:

Proposal 1

It is urgently desirable that a core curriculum for EE should be formulated for junior secondary education, which will include elements of science, technology and social education.

Proposal 2

In senior secondary education, it is desirable that the level of EE should be related to the problems and connections expounded in the WCS. For this reason analysis and adaptation of the WCS is necessary.

This would mean that a target final level of attainment in EE would be formulated for all pupils and especially for pupils going on to higher vocational and university education, some of whom, it is to be expected, will certainly be part of that group of people who not only influence their own behaviour but also that of others.

This is all very fine, but if these target levels are to become a reality, they must be translated into instruction that can really be put into practice. The question is therefore: how should you plan your instruction so that the target levels can be achieved? This brings me to the question of the organisation of the subject matter of EE.

ORGANISATION OF THE SUBJECT MATTER OF EE

My comments on the organisation of the subject matter of EE relate both the organisation of subject matter in the classroom and its organisation over years. As regards organisation over years, my comments will be in the nature of 'this first, that not until later.'

There are good reasons for this. Firstly, it obviously depends on the amount of time available for environmental topics - within the various subjects - in the different years.

Secondly - and this is more fundamental - you cannot regard pupils as vessels into which 'good' knowledge is poured; you must regard them as people who already have some knowledge and skills in all fields, these knowledge and skills determining to a large extent what they are able to learn at a given moment. Pupils structure their world from the knowledge they possess.

This view brings me to the so-called constructivist learning theories (of Ausubel, Gagne and others); I oppose the view that pupils can simply learn what is offered to them. That leads to parrot-fashion learning; given the objectives I have just formulatd, it is not good enough.

Piaget's idea that age-linked phases can be distinguished in children's cognitive development is now largely considered to have been superseded.

There are no theories in existence from which it can reasonably reliably be deduced what material can be offered to pupils at a given age. Research findings indicate that what pupils can learn depends more on the knowledge and skills they have already acquired than on their age (Novak, 1978).

Organisation of Subject Matter at Micro and Macro Levels

Before considering a number of consequences of this more thoroughly, it will be appropriate to explain in greater detail the difference between organisation of subject matter at classroom level and at the level of organisation over years.

In my opinion, organisation of subject matter at classroom level (the micro level) should be such that the pupils' learning processes with regard to specific subject matter should be able to progress as well as possible. The subject matter which is offered and the texts and workbooks or whatever may be used in this connection have a function in the teaching/learning process. By contrast, organisation of subject matter at the level of organisation over years - the curriculum (the macro level) - is concerned with what new subject matter is introduced successively during the different years, and possibly, what final levels of attainment must thereby be achieved. The organisation of the subject matter which is contained in the curriculum is thus related not to the way in which pupils' learning processes progress but to an increasing degree of complexity of what is taught, whether it be a question of knowledge or of skills or of both.

In other words, a constructivist point of reference has repercussions at both the micro and macro levels.

At the micro level it is therefore a question of how specific subject matter can be taught so that the learning process progresses as well as possible, whereas in the case of organisation of subject matter at the macro level it is a question of how the complexity of the material offered can increase, with the pupils' learning processes only important to the extent that they have consequences for the material taught to given years.

Criteria for Organisation of Subject Matter

Four criteria for the organisation of subject matter can be derived from constructivist theories. The first two relate to the micro level, and the third to the micro and the macro levels and the fourth to the macro level alone.

The first criterion is:

Structure the teaching/learning process in such a way that it links up with pupils' preconceptions or alternative frameworks, or that the pupils can bridge the gap between their preconceptions and what is taught.

This criterion sounds simpler than it really is. What should you do as a teacher if all your pupils have their own alternative frameworks? You can regard it mainly as a problem of subject matter. That consequently leads to the idea that you must know the pupils' preconceptions in order to be able to link up with them or to expose them as being invalid, i.e. misconceptions. In recent years a great deal of research has been done into pupils' preconceptions (see Pfundt & Duit, 1985, for an overview), but hardly any research of this kind relating to concepts important for EE has been published.

But you can also regard the problem as mainly one of communication, the question being: how do you persuade pupils that their alternative conceptions must be revised or at the very least that they need broadening? There is as yet little literature on how you should structure the teaching process if pupils are to revise and/or broaden their alternative conceptions. The available literature (see especially Novak & Gowin, 1984; Nussbaum & Novick, 1982; Driver & Oldham, 1985) indicates that it is or may be important to:

- create situations in which pupils are invited to state

and explain their ideas, preferably working in a group;

- create situations in which new solutions must be generated by pupils to solve 'problems'.

It is clear that these types of organisation of subject matter obviously cannot be practised for all EE subject matter. This is anyway not necessary; in my view it is only necessary for a number of essential EE concepts ('key concepts').

The second criterion is as follows:

It must be borne in mind when structuring the teaching /learning process that the extent to which pupils can perceive and can act in a 'problem solving' way is to a very large extent determined by the conceptual structure which they have at their command.

I am implying by this that a number of skills to a very great extent have a cognitive basis. This will not surprise you, I think, in view of the EE objectives which I have just presented. In fact, I also maintain that perception is influenced by theory. Let me give an example of this. A few years ago a colleague told me the following story. In a geography lesson, slides on Indonesia were shown. The left-hand side of the class were given an accompanying text which emphasised what a wonderful country Indonesia was. The right-hand side of the class were given a text which concentrated on the effects of colonial rule. Both groups thought they had been given the same text. In the class discussion which ensued the spokesmen for each group were able to show little understanding of each other's point of view.

This criterion for organisation of subject matter cannot be based on cognitivistic theories alone. Since Popper and Kuhn there has been unanimous criticism of empiricist ideas: the mere collecting of empirical facts does not logically lead to deeper insight or to new theory. The consequence of this is that to offer 'problem situations' - I mean 'problem solving' in the wide sense, as the application of what has been learned in practical situations - does not of itself lead to the solution of problem situations.

If the final objective is to solve problem t^1 (see Fig.1), it cannot be assumed that successive solving of problems p^1 to s^1 will be lead to the solving of problem t^1, or that the solving of p^1 will lead to the development of structure q which is necessary for the solving of q^1, etc. When it comes to the solving of problem t^1, the question if how pupils are to be able to develop cognitive structure t. An example: if we are concerned to analyse problem situations in which biological equilibrium plays a part, it is particularly important that system theory, from which the concept 'biological equilibrium' is derived, should be taught before any attempt is made to solve these problems, and it cannot be assumed that pupils will learn the theory needed in order to solve these problems by solving simpler problem situations (e.g. concerning relationships in food chains).

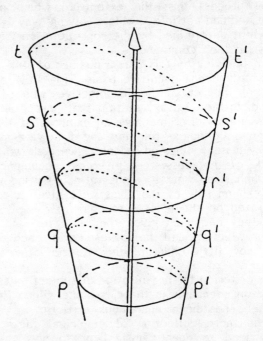

Figure 3:1   The development of cognitive structure t, which is necessary for the solution of problem t^1.

This brings me to a third criterion for organisation of subject matter, one which relates to the building up of theories:

We should try to develop theory from concrete objects and phenomena; it must be borne in mind that this development is discontinuous. (See Fig. 2).

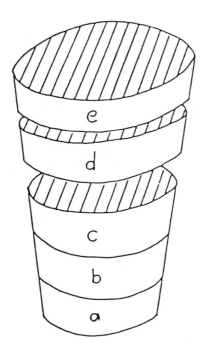

Figure 3.2   Discontinuous   development   of   abstract concepts

An increasing number of educational psychologists make a distinction between concrete concepts, though these are not always called concepts, and abstract concepts (e.g. Davydov, 1984). Concrete concepts are to be thought of as labels for things or descriptions of relations between things. Different designations may be used for the same object. I can designate a certain object as a 'flowering bush' or as an 'organism'; both designations may be correct, though the first is fairly specific and the second very general. The following levels, ranging from very concrete to general, may be distinguished:

a. specific designation of objects, phenomena and relations between them;

b. general designation of objects, phenomena and relations between them;

c. natural laws relating to objects, phenomena and relations between them.

Abstract concepts are concepts which have been derived from theories; i.e. a series of statements about objects, phenomena and relations between them which has the aim of explaining natural laws governing objects, phenomena and relations between them.

Bertalanffy's general system theory is an example of this. In many cases further theories of a greater degree of abstraction or validity can be formulated.

Theories are based on paradigms which cannot be logically derived from the natural laws which they deal with. This brings me back to philosophy of knowledge and criticism of empiricism.

I am aware that the foregoing may seem rather theoretical. I shall try to illustrate the levels I have just outlined with an example:

a. a description of how much grain a mouse (concrete) eats (e.g. on the basis of a study carried out by a group of pupils in class);

b. a statement such as: mice eat an average of x grammes of grain per day;

c. a statement such as: rodents eat vegetable food;

d. the statement: rodents and the plants which they eat, together with many other organisms, are part of an ecosystem which has a certain equilibrium;

e. the statement: organisms are part of developing systems which are characterised by lack of equilibrium (dynamic system - non-equilibrium (Jantsch, 1983)).

Or the statement: organisms form part of the energy flows within the ecosystem.[4]

Statements about systems do not follow directly from generalisations on food relationships and for this purpose a theoretical concept is introduced; statements about theoretical characteristics of systems cannot be deducted directly from the system concept itself, and for this purpose another abstract concept is needed which may be used on a new paradigm.

In teaching, the route from a to e must be travelled, so that a, b and c are introduced to younger pupils and d and e only to older pupils. But even with the older pupils, if a new theory is being introduced, the route to e must first be travelled.

This criterion for the organisation of EE is thus relevant both at macro level - the curriculum - and at micro level. This is illustrated in Figure 3.

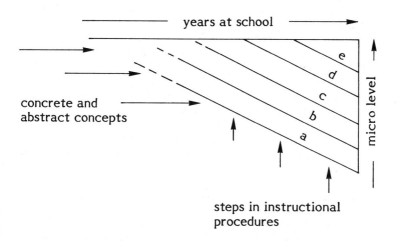

Figure 3.3   From concrete (a) to abstract (e)

The horizontal arrows indicate the extent to which concrete and abstract concepts can form part of the curriculum over the different years, with the higher arrows applying more to higher ability groups and the lower ones to lower ability groups and out-of-school activities in which the emphasis is placed on experience of nature.

The vertical lines indicate which steps can be taken successively in concrete teaching situations.

(If pupils have acquired a lot of concrete experience, steps a and b can largely be skipped.)

Two closely interconnected criteria for EE subject matter organisation follow from the objectives which I have formulated and from the hierarchy of systems in which human beings participate.

These objectives are:

- teaching learners to see how they can influence the elements of the systems they belong to and how they, in turn, are influenced by the other elements (human, biotic, abiotic);

- teaching learners to see how they can use their influence in the systems they belong to, taking account of the desired effects on the other elements in those systems and the continued existence of those systems as such. I hope it is clear that the objectives:

- in general relate to a hierarchy of organisational levels, ranging from the object level (e.g. influencing the organism) to the biosphere; and

- in particular relate to a hierarchy of systems to which human beings belong, ranging from the family to the world.

I wish to derive a criterion for EE subject matter organisation from both of these points. The first criterion is as follows:

It is necessary for organisational levels to be taught following an ascending hierarchy and for characteristics of systems at the various organisational levels to be introduced before there is any discussion of how these systems themselves are influenced and exert influence on other systems.

Young pupils can very easily learn to be aware that a hierarchy of sets (elements/systems) can be formulated, in which either the set is in turn an element of a higher-order set or the set can gradually be expanded. In the first class in secondary schools the theory of sets is often taught as part of the maths syllabus. The great difficulty, however, is to realise that higher-order systems have other characteristics than the elements of those systems; this applies particularly when we are dealing with the step from the object level to the 'super object' level: i.e. the step from the level in which an object is the system to a level in which the same objects are elements. In fact this is a 'white box' problem: how can you distinguish between systems if you cannot see them as systems? To be able to do so it is necessary to have mastered the 'system' concept. For the sake of clarity I have summarised this in the following diagram (Figure 4).

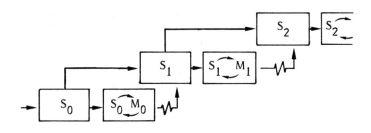

S_0 = system organisation level O
M_0 = environment of system S_0

Figure 3.4   Organisation of systems of different organisational levels and transitions from organisational levels 0 to 1 and 1 to 2. The zigzag arrow indicates that mastery of the system concept is necessary for an understanding of this step.

The second criterion which I derive from the EE objectives relates to the systems of which people individually form a part. This criterion can be seen as a special case of the previous one, in view of its formulation. The argument behind it is different, however. It goes as follows:

Systems to which pupils belong an individuals must be taught following an ascending hierarchy.

The objectives which I have proposed are, as I have already said, partly directed towards strengthening the sense of identity. Insight into the way in which influence is exerted can make an important contribution (particularly, of course, if it is a case of influence by or on persons, objects or organisms which are important to the individual in question). In the case of systems which are higher up in the hierarchy or are more all-embracing, it is difficult to see that you as an individual have any influence; therefore it seems desirable to introduce systems to which pupils belong, starting with the ones in which there is likely to be the greatest insight and progressing to those in which there is likely to be less insight. In the case of systems in which individuals have little influence, insight into how those systems are maintained in existence is of great importance for showing how you yourself, perhaps unwittingly, co-operate in upholding the rules or natural laws of those systems.

Insight into how the exerting of influence works can be significantly increased if the system concept is understood. I therefore propose a repetition of the proposed organisation. (Figure 5a).

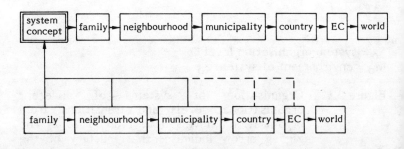

Figure 3.5a Organisation of systems to which human beings belong, with introduction at a given moment of the system concept.

I would comment at this stage that it is not clear to me how far it is sensible to try to explain pupils' influence without having introduced the system concept.

That is why I have indicated the connection between the more all-embracing systems and the system concept with a broken line.

This does not mean, of course, that the teaching may not deal with aspects of the EC or the world before this stage is reached.

On the contrary, it is highly desirable in my view that aspects of more all-embracing and hierarchically higher systems should be introduced in concrete terms before the influence of the pupils themselves in those systems is dealt with. Figure 5a can therefore be expanded to Figure 5b.

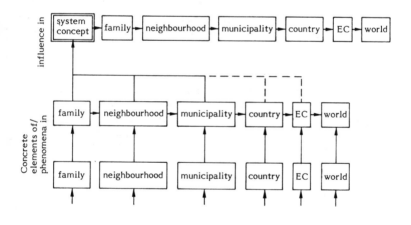

Figure 3.5b   Organisations of systems to which human beings belong, in three steps: concrete elements/phenomena, individual influence and introduction of the system concept.

CONCLUSIONS AND SOME MORE RECOMMENDATIONS

In this paper I have made some recommendations as to the form and content of EE objectives and as to the organisation of EE subject matter at micro and macro levels.

I then made some proposals (in 2.3) for a future EE core curriculum. My expectation is that a core curriculum for junior secondary education for the years to come will be developed in the Netherlands by the SLO.

My second proposal related to the conversion of the WCS into a core curriculum for senior secondary education. This has not yet been done and, moreover, I know of no plans made by groups or individuals intending to do so in the near future.

I would like to round off my argument with two supplementary recommendations:

Proposal 3
It is desirable that in the fairly near future not only should an EE core curriculum be developed for junior secondary education but also a longitudinal core curriculum for 4- to 16-year-olds. This development is urgently needed if the goals of EE are to be realised.

Proposal 4
It is gradually becoming time to mark out a teaching methodology for EE. This must contain statements about objectives, subject matter organisation, teaching processes, general organisation and peripheral conditions. Recourse must therefore be had to those educational and pedagogical theories which are supported by empirical findings, since - if I am allowed to choose - I would rather aim for success than mere good intentions.

NOTES

1. Thanks are due to D.A. Huitzing for commenting on and editing this article.
2. I assume that teachers and other educators are paid to exert influence in a desired direction.
3. In addition, of course, systems with a higher level of abstraction can also be distinguished, for example energy system and economic systems: such systems are not covered by the objectives mentioned above.

4. Statements about systems which do not refer to concrete characteristics of objects - such as energy or the economy - belong to category e.

BIBLIOGRAPHY

Bertalanffy, L. von (1968). General System Theory. Braziller, New York.

Davydov, V.V. (1984). 'Substantial generalisation and the dialectic-materialistic theory of thinking.' In: M. Hedegard, P. Ilakkarainen & Y. Engestrom (editors). Learning and teaching on a scientific basis, methodological and epistemological aspects of the activity theory of learning and teaching. Aarhus Universitet, Psykologisk Institut.

Driver, R & V. Oldham (1985). 'A constructivist approach to curriculum development in science.' Paper for symposium 'Personal Construction of Meaning in Educational Settings', BERA, Sheffield, 1985.

Festinger, L. (1957). A theory of cognitive dissonance. Stanford University Press, Stanford, California.

de Groot, A.D. (1978). 'Wat neemt de leerling mee van onderwijs? Gedragsrepertoires, programma's, kennis en vaardigheden.' (What does the pupil get from education? Behaviour repertoires, programmes, knowledge and skill). Handboek Onderwijspraktijk (Manual of teaching practice), 2.3.Gro.A1 - 2.3.Gro.A.23.

International Union for the Conservation of Nature and Natural Resources (IUCN) (1980). World Conservation Strategy.

Jantsch, E. (1983). The self-organising universe. Pergamon Press, Oxford/New York.

Novak, J.D. (1978). 'An Alternative to Piagetian Psychology for Science and Mathematics Education.' Studies in Science Education, 5, 1-30.

Novak, J.D. & D.B. Gowin (1984). Learning how to learn. Cambridge University Press, Cambridge/London/New York.

Nussbaum, J. & S. Novick (1982). 'Alternative Frameworks, conceptual conflict and accommodation: toward a principled teaching strategy.' Instructional Science 11, 183-200.

Pfundt, H. & R. Duit (1985). Bibliography. Students' Alternative Frameworks and Science Education. Institut fur die Padagogik der Naturwissenschaften. IPN, Kurzberichte, 31.

Watslawick, P., J.H. Beavin, D.D. Jackson (1967). Pragmatics of Human Communications. Norton & Co., Inc., New York.

Chapter Four

THE RESPONSE TO ENVIRONMENTAL PROBLEMS

V. Sokolov and S. Khromov

ENVIRONMENTAL EDUCATION

Environmental Education (EE) in schools in the USSR is part of the general education. Students are taught the fundamental principles of the interaction between nature and society and acquire some practical skills. EE is integral, interdisciplinary and socially-orientated. To make school children aware of the responsibility for the environment means to make them realise the relationship between man and society and the need for an ecological behaviour that is consistent with the interests of society they live in. It is essential that school be oriented towards two social objectives. The first goal is to foster the sense of responsibility for the state of the environment that they must observe in all aspects of their personal and social behaviour. The second goal is to teach them practical skills in how to monitor the environment, protect it, improve it, and foster an intolerance of carelessness and wastefulness in respect to nature. This objective can hardly be achieved without the general involvement of students in the active movement for a better environment. Though these goals are separate, they may go hand in hand in the educational process.

The need for an interdisciplinary approach in EE is recognised by an overwhelming majority of specialists, including school teachers. The best way of implementing the concept is, however, still open to discussion. In the USSR different pilot projects are launched in order to elaborate a comprehensive interdisciplinary programme which would provide guidelines for EE programmes for each subject taught at school.

Accepting the concept of an interdisciplinary EE some Soviet educationists have seen the need for a successive generalisation and recapitulation of ecological knowledge at different stages of education, including that of the school level. Specifically, they point to the importance of 'junctions of integration' of environmental knowledge. Different methods can be employed to achieve this aim at different phases and stages of the same level. Among them are the 'interdisciplinary classes' when team-teaching approach is used; 'debating classes' attended by specialists who deal with specific environmental problems; imitations and role games; different kinds of field studies which help students apply in practice what they have learnt and display initiative. There is also a special integrated course for senior students. The course is designed to integrate the relatively fragmented information available to students from sources in different subjects into a single whole, and to bring into focus the environmental problems at the national and global levels.

An integrated course of this kind does not detract from the interdisciplinary nature of the general approach. The summing up and generalisation of information at the final stage of schooling combined with periodic integration of knowledge received in the process of general education would undoubtedly help to create a comprehensive picture of the environmental problems and develop students' abilities to solve them.

The out-of-class and out-of-school environmental activities are very important as well. Usually they are carried out by school teachers and by non-school institutions. The Soviet Union has wide experience in this field. It was in the 1920s and 30s when different biology and nature clubs started their activities at schools and pioneer palaces. They continue to operate. The All-Union arrangements such as, for example, 'Day of Birds', etc. are carried out annually. At the same time new forms of activities appear, the school forests, 'blue' and 'green' patrols, small forestry academies, ecology stations, groups to combat soil erosion etc. School forestry groups help pupils to choose a career. Many of them enter forestry institutes, or take jobs in forestry. Children do really understand that their actions help to conserve nature. Groups to combat soil erosion, for example, inspect the district, mark on a map the areas needing protection, carry out tree planting and collect the seeds of grasses to prevent erosion. 'Blue patrol' groups take part in the All-Union activity called 'Living Silver'. Pupils mark on a map places where fish may gather in spring, and carry out activities to save fish. They also study flora and fauna in local reservoirs, keep them clean and stage campaigns against poaching.

Most of the students at the small forestry academies

are 14-15 years old. They study at the academy for three years. When studying for the second and third year all students have their own scientific instructor and an individual plan of work. To complete each year of study, students present the results of their scientifically-based investigation in written form. Upon graduation they get a diploma, a description of their abilities and behaviour, and a recommendation to enter a Forestry Institute to continue their education.

This system of special secondary technical and vocational schools faces its own specific problems. Depending on areas of specialisation students have to tackle concrete environmental problems using a problem-solving approach and leaving considerable room for participation. For technical schools the following three basic trends in EE may be singled out:

- incorporation of environmental problems in the syllabuses of traditional subjects;

- special/professional environmental training;

- practical and social activities of students.

Thus, EE at the level of secondary and special secondary schools ensures a stage-by-stage formation of students' attitude towards the environment. The first stage is to foster the attitude of personal identification with the environmental problems. This is the stage of knowledge accumulation in the fields of natural and social sciences, economics, history and technical subjects. The decision stage, however, involves the development of practical skills in environmental protection and rational use of natural resources. The latter can be achieved only through personal practical experience.

Soviet specialists agree that the most realistic alternative to improve the content of school education is not to overburden it with new additional data on the man-society-nature relationships (though some additions might be justified), but to concentrate on the concept of the integral nature of the environment at different levels within the biosphere.

UNIVERSITY LEVEL AND BEYOND

Owing to the complex character and the novelty of EE problems it is often necessary to first carry out experiments in some universities or institutes to show new possible methods of education and prove their efficiency. For a number of years, for example, Soviet specialists discussed the problem of whether it was necessary to introduce the speciality 'ecology' (in order to train professional ecologists) at the university or not. It is not yet clear whether the national economy needs these professionals with such a broad outlook, or whether they should concentrate on specific environmental problems, e.g. in industry, transport, etc. Opinions still differ, and that is why it was decided to keep on experimenting in Kazan and Sverdlovsk universities.

The EE at the tertiary level is continuous, multi- and interdisciplinary and integrated. It is differentiated in terms of occupational orientation. There is a trend of incorporation of ecology principles in all the study courses. Environmental training is peculiar to all three stages/forms of education in Soviet universities and institutes:

(a) acquisition of a general professional background;

(b) specialisation;

(c) in-depth study of a particular field within the chosen specialisation.

EE at the tertiary level is considered to be most effective when it is based on a standard interdepartmental (interdisciplinary) programme that takes into account the field of specialisation. Such a programme envisages the study of the general environmental problems within the framework of an 'introduction-into-the-speciality' course, and courses on social sciences which outline the philosophical aspects of the nature-society relationships and incorporate a 'nature conservation' course. In a number of universities and colleges 'Nature Conservation' has been taught since 1948. At present it is read in over 90% of universities and institutes. It takes up 10-36 teaching periods depending on the future professional occupation of students. The programme, which involves practical activities, also covers the economics of natural resources, and the ecological aspects of specific academic subjects related

82

to the general professional background and specialisation. Much attention is given to the final phase of this comprehensive programme - where there is an evaluation of proposed decisions. This is done to test the economic feasibility and ecological safety of the project or the process.

Specialists are also trained in diverse specific fields of environmental science and practice. For example, in the early eighties, Soviet universitities, institutes and secondary special technical and vocational schools trained specialists in the following fields:

- rational use of natural resources and protection of environment (for studies qualified in 'biology' and 'geography');

- ecology and more efficient use of natural resources;

- rational use of water resources and decontamination of industrial dicharges;

- water supply, sewage and waste water purification;

- water supply in agriculture, water supply development and protection of water resources;

- ichthyology and pisciculture;

- forestry;

- the use of gas and fuel oil and air protection (for students specialising in 'heat and power engineering');

- waste reprocessing and recycling;

- hygiene, sanitation and epidemiology;

- architectural ecology;

- construction ecology.

Extensive involvement of students, graduates and post-graduates in research programmes carried out by laboratories in institutes and universities opens up additional possibilities. Students are given opportunities to acquire specific practical skills and theoretical backgrounds, and, what is most important, to gain experience in dealing with concrete environmental problems. It is also essential that this work is conducted chiefly by a teaching staff, competent and experienced both in research and training.

Today, over 350 institutes and universities in the Soviet Union are involved in research into some 1,300 important environmental projects. Some two-thirds of all research projects are related to improvements of processing techniques and protection of water, land resources and the atmosphere from pollution. The programmes that concern the protection of biological resources come second. The third developmental trend involves the socio-economic problems of environment. All these activities are co-ordinated by specifially assigned institutes or universities.

The training of school teachers is rather a specific field of EE activities. Two problems are outstanding. The first is to ensure a general EE background for teachers of different subjects; and the second is to train specialist teachers in EE. Teacher training differs from the training of students at other institutes. The aim of teacher training institutes is, first and foremost, to train educators who will be able both to teach and socialise youth. Consequently, the EE of potential teachers must be different and broader in scope.

In Soviet teacher training institutes, the environmental problems are not taught as a separate subject. Teachers of all school subjects are trained now in this field. This provides an opportunity to realise the interdisciplinary objective at the secondary school level. Various measures are designed to enhance the social activities of potential teachers. Out-of-class activities and optional studies offer a very good chance to encourage pupils' interests in the conservation of nature. In this connection, much attention is devoted to the training in the methods and techniques of such activities to make them appealing and entertaining. Many teacher training institutes run special activities programmes, which are open to any student interested in these problems.

Some teacher training institutes in the Soviet Union organise special theoretical, practical and optional courses and seminars on environmental problems. However, and it has been repeatedly pointed out at international meetings by representatives of many other countries, EE for teachers fails to meet modern requirements. This problem is still very urgent and needs a solution. A failure to do so would have the most grave consequences, as teachers are directly responsible for the education of the future generation. It was this problem which prompted the decision adopted at an All-Union Conference in Minsk to introduce a new compulsory course 'Nature Conservation' in the curricula of all departments of teacher training institutes.

Another possibility for environmental teacher training is provided by a system of refresher courses. The ample opportunities in this system are widely used for training other specialists as well. The following two basic trends can be distinguished:

1. a refresher course proper, i.e. a course designed to inform specialists, managers, educators/teachers, etc. of new developments and achievements in science and engineering relevant to their activities, to bring their knowledge and understanding up to date;

2. actual re-training of specialists, managers and educators/teachers, i.e. provision of instruction in new trends and areas of environmental activities.

Unlike refresher training, the system of re-training is largely oriented to deal with strategic problems, i.e. with radical changes in the attitude towards the environment and the use of its resources. In many countries re-training is handled by special departments of the universities or institutes. The same is true in the USSR, where these courses last 5-6 months as a full-time educational facility. Among those who attend these courses are the specialists, scientists, educators, decision makers and managers. Participants are offered a course in 'Ecology and More Efficient Use of the Natural Resources' (wasteless production, purification of waste waters, gas and dust emissions, environmental monitoring, etc.).

To conclude this brief discussion of general trends in EE at the university level we need to stress the following points:

- The problem of training highly-skilled EE personnel for both the school and the post-school levels is still very urgent;

- The general methodological principles of EE must be defined more accurately for relevant training of

85

students in all specialities;

- These principles can underlie specific methodological recommendations for standard EE programmes and comprehensive syllabuses for all specialities;

- Simultaneous efforts should be applied in order to make general EE courses more specific and problem oriented.

NON-FORMAL EE

The potential of non-formal EE is enormous. It is non-formal EE that shapes public opinion and the response to local, regional and global environmental problems. It stimulates the direct participation of the public in outdoor nature conservation activities and increases the efficiency of these endeavours. There is a comprehensive well-integrated non-formal system of EE in the USSR. Nature conservation societies in the Soviet republics have become really mass-scale organisations. The main tasks of their activities are as follows:

- dissemination of knowledge of the environment;

- cultivation in people of a responsible attitude towards, and love for, nature;

- attracting the public into work to conserve nature.

The nature conservation societies have a membership of some 40 million and have primary organisations at industrial enterprises, on collective and state farms and in other establishments. At schools and educational institutions the courses of public lectures (so-called people's universities) on nature conservation do a great deal towards disseminating knowledge of nature and teaching methods of protecting the environment. At present more than 1,500 people's universities are functioning in the USSR.

A variety of public agencies are involved in non-formal EE. Most active among these are the following:

- various volunteer organisations (nature conservation societies, educational agencies, nature lovers' societies and clubs, e.g. wildlife, horticulture clubs, etc.);

- out-of-school student organisations (school forests, ecological stations, forest academies, clubs, student
  ecological societies, etc.);

- scientific societies (geographical, zoological, etc.);

- people's or 'open' universities;

- museums, specifically museums of regional ethno-
  graphy;

- houses of nature;

- nature reserves and national parks.

Among the various forms and methods of public EE the
following can be mentioned: mass media (newspapers, magazines, radio and TV); audio-visual aids (films, slides, mobile
and stationary exhibits, posters, dioramas, etc.); books,
pamphlets and other publications; study tours and excursions; imitation and role games, lectures and discussions.

Special mention should be of the growing educational
activities of national parks and nature/biosphere reserves. It
is a well known fact that the international network of
biosphere reserves is rapidly expanding, and the relevant
MAB (UNESCO Programme 'Man and the Biosphere') project
No. 8-A is assuming central importance.

As the human impact on the environment increases, the
nature reserves offer the only chance for many to come into
contact with a relatively unspoiled nature. No visual aid or
description, however good, can do better than involvement
in the real environment.

The type of EE carried out in nature reserves is not
strictly formal or non-formal. Most important are the
opportunities and facilities provided by nature reserves
rather than various education activities of the personnel in
the reserves as such. The following six trends of EE in
nature reserves can be discerned:

- museum-type activities (indoor and outdoor);

- acquainting visitors with local scenic sights, landscape,
  flora and fauna;

- providing facilities for students' and specialists' field

practice;

- providing facilities for out-of-school work of pupils on nature conservation;

- publishing, lecturing and EE through mass media;

- implementation in practice of the principles of socio-ecodevelopment.

At the same time EE activities in nature reserves have certain negative aspects. Crowds of visitors, even though most of them stay in the buffer zones only, increase the anthropogenic pressure on nature in the reserves significantly. Besides the necessity to cope with a constant flow of visitors means that many staff-members are diverted from their main duties, which are to conduct research and monitoring.

The unique EE facilities of nature reserves are beyond doubt even if the objectives and forms of EE there have yet to be explicitly formulated. Nature reserves have acccumulated vast and valuable research experience, a solid research base and highly-skilled research personnel, i.e. all the necessary pre-requisites for effective training of specialists. The aesthetic value of surroundings of landscapes, biotopes, plants and animals for demonstration in the special reserve zones; lectures, talks and study courses at indoor and outdoor museums; discussions at seminars, conferences, etc. make the effort to educate the population very effective from the scientific and emotional points of view and bring people close to nature.

CONCLUSIONS

To make EE successful co-ordination is necessary at all levels. In the Soviet Union, for instance, the functions of such a co-ordinating agency are exercised by the Section on EE set up within the system of the State Committee on Science and Technology, a year after the Tbilisi Conference (1977). The 50 members of the Section are the leading scholars, scientists, specialists, teachers and decision-makers. Yet, no matter how successfully problems of environment and EE are handled in one country, even as large as the Soviet Union, there is still a need for a global approach and international co-ordination.

The UNESCO-UNEP International Programme of EE is an example of successful co-operation in this area. Since 1975, pursuant to Recommendation 96 of the UN Conference on the Human Environment (Stockholm, 1972), principles developed in the Belgrade Charter (1975) and Recommendations of the Tbilisi Conference (1977), UNESCO and UNEP have jointly undertaken a vast EE programme. Effective co-operation between different states and international organisations resulted in good progress of this programme. As a result of it, the international community succeeded in introducing EE at different levels of education, especially the training of highly qualified environmentalists.

But not all possible avenues have been explored. We have to improve the process of exchange of experience, and seek new forms of it. In this connection the initiative of the USSR Academy of Sciences (V.E. Sokolov) to open the study courses at the biology faculty of the Moscow State University for the environmental training of specialists from developing countries seems timely and promising.

The trends of EE, plans of future activities and the results of the work, that have been carried out during the last 10 years within the UNESCO-UNEP Programme, are to be discussed at the coming series of regional meetings and then at the International Conference 'Tbilisi + 10' in 1987. This will be an end to the first phase of the international programme and the start of the second phase. Some points should be emphasised in the second phase:

-   to give priority to EE, as key factor in the improvement of the environment;

-   to elaborate the concept of EE, and define its content;

-   to speed up and modernise the environmental training of teachers etc. for all the levels of education;

-   to declare as immediate tasks the following actions:

    (i)   to speed up the exchange of the environmental information and experience in solving of the environmental problems, especially between the developed and developing countries;

    (ii)   to develop programmes for elimination of eco-

89

logical illiteracy, first and foremost for rural populations.

(iii) to give attention to one of the most significant objectives of EE, i.e. the peace struggle, anti-nuclear protests, arms race limitation, etc.

International co-operation in EE is particularly important today, when the world political situation has deteriorated. Problems of detente, limitation of the arms race and disarmament are not adequately represented in EE and are frequently neglected as irrelevant. This attitude is entirely wrong. It is a well known fact that wars, and especially modern warfare, destroy the environment. But not only direct hostilities are ecologically dangerous. The environment is damaged by continuing nuclear tests and other military activities which are threatening to spread into outer space. These activities are also a heavy drain on manpower and natural resources. Budgets of both developed and developing countries suffer heavily from the arms race and military actions. Militarism is detrimental to international environmental co-operation, specifically, in respect of large-scale global and regional programmes and projects which require the joint efforts of many states and heavy investments.

The efficiency of human actions depends on the level of knowledge, in our case on the level of EE and the environmental awareness. Ecological implications of the military activities, the arms race and disarmament should be part of EE which, in its turn, must be forged into a new effective tool of mobilising social movements for peaceful co-existence, detente and ecodevelopment.

ENVIRONMENTAL EDUCATION IN THE USSR

MINISTRY OF EDUCATION

- Teacher Training Institutes
- Refreshing, Further Training, Institutes/ Faculties/ Courses
- Secondary Schools
- Pre-School Institutions

SCIENTIFIC COUNCIL ON EE

ACADEMY OF PEDAGOGIC SCIENCES

- Scientific Institutes on Problems of School Education
- Laboratory on EE

MINISTRY OF HIGHER AND SPECIAL SECONDARY EDUCATION

- Refreshing, Further Training, Re-training, Courses/ Faculties
- Universities Institutes, Special Secondary Colleges

TRADE/INDUSTRIAL MINISTRIES

STATE COMMITTEE ON VOCATIONAL AND TECHNICAL EDUCATION

- Vocational and Technical Colleges/Schools

NON-FORMAL EE

- Mass media, Out-of-school organisations, Clubs, Societies, People's Universities

SECTION ON EE

INTERNATIONAL CO-OPERATION

- UNESCO National Commission, UNEP National Commission, MAB National Committee, CMEA, IUCN Commission on Education

Chapter Five

OPEN LEARNING AND TEAM-WORKING: A PERSPECTIVE FROM THE YOUTH ORGANISATIONS

Jan J. Voordouw

INTRODUCTION

Perhaps the most common and the most intensive way of learning is through self-education. This holds also for learning to know nature and to understand environmental dilemmas. Many people experience nature and environment in a practical way or read about it, because they consider it interesting. They develop a scheme of terms of reference through the many types of information which society offers.

As long as the school system does not provide sufficient integration of subjects and suffers from an unfortunate lack of links with everyday reality, environmental education in school in seriously hampered. Also, school education stimulates mainly the personal achievements of the student and not so much the seeking of solutions as a group. In most situations, a basic feeling for and understanding of the complex web of inter-relations between nature and society has to be gained through a large input of out-of-school experience.

This article focusses on the non-formal dimension of education. It is based on my experiences in youth environmental action at local, national as well as international levels. The article refers regularly to the International Youth Federation for Environmental Studies and Conservation (IYF), the only organisation which unites youth environmental groups worldwide. Environmental education is a major aspect of the programmes of IYF.

For illustration, a range of examples are taken up. The cases chosen are all from Europe, because that is the region I am most familiar with.

BETTER SELF-EDUCATION? TEAM-WORKING!

Much non-formal education is done by people themselves for themselves, true self-education, by reading, studying nature, etc. Many young people are so much interested in the environment, that for instance, they take all opportunities to go out and observe birds, or plants, or read everything they can find about tigers, water pollution or geology. Some of them will evolve into real specialists.

But doing things in a group multiplies the advantageous effects with regard to effective learning, acquiring skills and achieving results. Groups of volunteers (consumer and community groups, youth groups) make in this way a very positive contribution to society. Everybody, but especially young people, is continuously building up their personal perception of the world. Together in such a public interest group, a horizontal - open - learning situation emerges. This is at least for environmental education (most probably also for many other types of education) a much better learning situation than the vertical - closed - one, with a teacher or leader and a group of people to be taught.

In such open learning systems, society is reflected. Members give and receive. Everybody has his or her own set of knowedge and skills and will use it to the best capacity. Working and learning together requires quite some inter-action: discussion about each other's ideas, the use of each person's potential as optimally as possible, decisions on the functional division in the group, etc.

Communication, the passing on of experience and information, is a basic feature of such a group, and necessary for team-working. To give each member of a team a task is not enough. The old saying that 'a union is more than the parts' means also that each one needs enough insight into the other tasks. In a volunteer group, especially in the youth group, this means that everybody needs to know more or less about everything going on. Therefore, team-working requires a communication web to better serve education.

YOUTH ENVIRONMENTAL ORGANISATIONS

Young people pursue environmental activities in a wide variety of youth organisations. Scouts, Guides and Pioneer movements have been helping young people to appreciate their environment for most of this century. Youth organisa-tions promoting outdoor recreation, such as hiking and youth hostelling, often include in their programme a large element of conservation. Clubs for observation and conservation of wildlife exist nearly everywhere, either as independent youth organisations or as junior sections of adult societies. Special conservation corps of young volunteers have been formed to undertake practical tasks in managing and restoring the environment. Young people work in community service projects to improve living conditions, in health and agriculture. Environmental groups are often formed by students of relevant disciplines, attached to universities and colleges. There are also organisations which provide young people with the opportunity for scientific research, usually associated with schools.

Some of the groups as listed here have only a peripheral interest in environmental conservation, but others have it as their main objective. In the latter group we can distinguish two different organisational structures: first, the more traditional self-governing conservation-youth organisations (by 'self-governing' is meant: run by young people), second, the specialist environmental action organisations. Amongst students both types occur more or less equally.

INVOLVEMENT IN COMMUNITY ACTION

Youth can and do play vital roles in what is perhaps the most important level of environmental activities: the community. These roles embrace education, training and public action. Youth movements, including youth environment movements, are often not highly specialised and gather many different views and activities. Enthusiastic initiatives almost immediately get a chance to be recognised, under the motto: 'If you'd like something new in your organisation, do it yourself!'. The principle of democratic learning ('everybody educates everybody') permeates all self-governing youth organisations. Within all activities, knowledge and experience is more or less diffusely passed on. It is vital to a youth group to be open, always willing to reach more people. If the circle becomes closed, the group will decline within a few years.

The general principle of democratic learning is expressed in many different ways. Often special working groups or study circles are formed (e.g. for bird watching, entomology, landscape planning or around protection of a certain area). They collect resource persons and interested new members on special subjects, but have also wider duties in the entire youth organisation, e.g. in training local groups. In some organisations special camps for new members are organised. Here new people are introduced to nature studies, protection, group life, etc. In many other organisations, a whole series of introductory camps on special branches of nature studies/protection or ecology are held annually. Participants will, after such a training, be able to introduce similar activities into their own local groups.

Excursions are basic to the programme of each naturalist group. They may be simply morning or afternoon walks in the neighbourhood, or longer whole-day excursions to interesting places at greater distance. The main purpose of an excursion is to observe the environment. But excursions to modern farming, nuclear plants or water purification installations can also be part of the programme.

Tree planting, construction work, clearing of rubbish, fencing, shrub clearance, reserve maintenance, sand dune reclamation, creation of footpaths and nature trails, etc. are also a successful part of the programme of many youth environmental organisations. Camps and courses are traditionally the main activity of many youth organisations, at local, regional, national and international levels. But also projects and surveys fulfil an important function in communities, always carried out with a high input of many members and a lot of enthusiasm. Examples of local surveys are the analysis of a locality which is changing due to human influence, observation of changing habitat and fauna over a period of years, measurements of pollution levels, enquiries among fishermen and other residents closely associated with the environment, etc. Some projects evolve into big activities with many other public organisations. As long as the information exchange runs well and an open web of communication is maintained, new people and new groups will feel easily involved: there is then the basis for team-working.

Activities of youth environmental organisations are supported by many meetings and seminars, and an incredible number of low-cost publications.

THE EARLY INTERNATIONAL YOUTH LEADER TRAINING COURSES

Since its start in 1956, the International Youth Federation for Environmental Studies and Conservation (IYF) has conducted and co-organised a yearly programme of international training courses for youth leaders. Many of these courses were held, originally in Europe, but later also in

Africa, Asia, the Pacific, South and Central America. The courses, held over many years and in many countries, have provided a lot of experience and resulted in a certain tradition or organisation and follow-up.

The concept of youth leader training courses originates from the 50s. In 1954, the General Assembly of the IUCN adopted a resolution to devote particular attention to the development of international camps and meetings for young people interested in nature conservation and landscape planning. This was worked out by youth environmental organisations from north-west Europe, in co-operation with the Society of the Nature Protection Park Luneburger Heide (FGR). In the period 1955-1968, annually a course was held at the international level, in the Luneburger Heide.

Aims were roughly to offer young people from environmental organisations possibilities to meet, to obtain a sound knowledge of European problems of nature conservation and landscape planning, through practical conservation tasks, nature studies and discussions, and in this way initiate future work for participants, when back home in their own countries.

In the first years, conservation work in the nature reserve was the main activity; lectures and excursions were held when time was left. In the following years, gradually a programme was built up. More attention was paid to world ecology, and conservation work in the protected area had to be stopped as it did not leave sufficient time for the training itself, and because it was felt necessary to visit and stay at different places during the course.

The participants, usually 20-25 girls and boys in the age group 17-28 years, came from 8-10 countries of Europe. Participants were accepted under the condition that they had already experience in environmental conservation and were prepared to co-operate actively in the programme. Each participant was requested to give a lecture on the main environmental problems in his/her country of origin and on his/her youth organisation and eventually other environmental organisations.

The entire course programme was discussed in detail at the first evening, but also on later occasions. Participants had always the opportunity to include special wishes/ideas.

As in many international meetings, understanding each other could cause problems. The official languages at the course were English and German. Interpreters were not available, but there were always some people who managed both languages so well that a translation could be improvised sufficiently. Once a Russian language group was organised: for the course leaders it was important to know how the individual participants managed to speak a foreign language. The first evening with short presentations of the participants was a good opportunity to investigate the different fluencies. During such a course, it is important to fight the fear of speaking foreign languages. The discussions were not to be made by fluent speakers only.

SPREADING OF THE COURSES

After 1968, no youth leader training courses were organised in the Luneburger Heide for six years. Meanwhile, the German Youth League for Nature Studies still organised several times an 'international camp' in the area, in co-operation with IYF.

In 1974, IYF decided to set up a new Luneburger Heide course, with an updated programme. Besides the traditional elements like ecology, field biology and the introduction to youth environmental work, the new programme included more on international institutions and programmes, Third World and environment, environmental strategies, public actions and awareness campaigns. This course was run at the Luneburger Heide in 1974 and 1975. After 1975 the courses spread out, and were held at different venues each year. Through the support of the European Youth Foundation (founded 1973), it became also possible to organise more than one course a year. Currently IYF-Europe organises three to four courses annually, besides co-organisation of numerous international camps.

In the 70s youth environmental organisations from other continents started to join the IYF network. Youth leader training courses were initiated outside Europe also. The first ones were held in India, Hong Kong and Kenya. Nowadays the IYF has grown into a real worldwide network, with a decentralised structure and youth leader training courses are being organised by youth environmental organisations all over the world. The 1986/87 programme covers courses in Nepal, Bangladesh, India, Tanzania, Ghana, Venezuela, Ireland, Cyprus, Portugal and Norway.

PRINCIPLES OF COURSES

A set of principles which has evolved over the years illustrates the success of this form of training. The courses are usually held for 7-14 days, cover a wide variety of topics, and are organised by some local youth groups. Usually 25-40 people attend, drawn from a variety of youth and student organisations. This number has proved to be the best. Not too many: it is still possible to learn at least everyone's name and face within a few days, which has multiple advantages for the running of the course. It is also vital to encourage contributions from the participants, whatever the extent of their experience. Not too few: the group still gathers a lot of experiences and may easily be split up in 4-8 small groups.

EDUCATIONAL ELEMENTS OF COURSES

International Youth Leader Training Courses usually draw participants from four to ten neighbouring countries. They are organised mainly by one or more local youth environmental organisations. In consequence the courses always support initiatives of youth organisations in a certain geographic region and mostly a great need is filled. Themes and detailed working methods originate from the networking in the specific region.

A very important purpose of each course is to offer young environmentalists an opportunity to meet enabling direct exchange of experiences. The courses are therefore basic for youth networking, youth environmental projects, joint public campaigns, etc. At courses, the programmes and projects of youth environmental groups receive a useful feedback from the participants and many new ideas which might be integrated. This makes the youth environmental movement more democratic and more effective as a whole.

The widely spread youth organisations have a relatively easy access to the public and media. Courses are often combined with a public action. This can be street theatre, quickly composed environmental songs, a small demonstration, workshops, exhibitions and fora for the public, a thematic 'town-trail', an excursion for the children, etc. Learning and doing is highly integrated.

Young environmentalists consider it of utmost important to pass on the attitude that 'we can change something together'. The understanding of principles of environment and development are improved during the course. The many ways by which young people can make an impact are shown, discussed and demonstrated. All this results in a much more active approach in public awareness campaigns, in which basic ecological knowledge and non-formal education techniques, which are always included in the course programme, are a valuable tool. The change to an active attitude results not only in improved programmes of youth environmental groups, but often also in the establishment of new youth or other environmental groups.

NATURE EXPEDITIONS

Numerous nature expeditions have been instrumental in building up international co-operation in the youth environmental movement. Regularly members of youth organisations decide to organise a nature expedition with participants from different youth environmental organisations, and often also drawn from different countries. Such experiences can be seen as extrapolations of nature studies and environmental activities executed in local groups. They are real holiday hiking exercises, organised in a very informal way. In fact the only thing on the programme is 'to explore an area'. This is in contrast to courses where the venue is mostly restricted to one building or camping site and where an elaborated programme exists for each day.

Thus, nature expeditions are not characterised by meetings, where certain subjects have to be discussed. They are not centred around a branch of nature- or environmental studies. Their objectives seem to be nothing more than having a nice hiking holiday together in nature.

Nature expeditions are a 24 hours per day experience in which young environmentalists walk and live closely together. They provide the best opportunities to familiarise each other about one's life, organisation, ideas, etc. There is a very open atmosphere.

An important difference from more formal meetings is that participants are not hampered by being representatives of organisations. They start with their own wishes, their own ideas, they speak mainly for themselves. Nevertheless a basis for joint projects, for networking is established; some people from different countries or organisations learn to know each other and decide to co-operate on certain issues. This might result in involvement of their organisations. The co-operation between individuals can be lifted to higher organisational levels.

In this way, communication between environmentalists at the grass roots level in an open-learning atmosphere, such as is provided in nature expeditions, means a significant strengthening of international co-operation. It generates new initiatives, but also backs existing efforts if they are found worthwhile. A continuous critical dialogue on the need for, advantages of, and elements of co-operation is maintained.

The IYF is built on the results of international courses, nature expeditions and youth exchange (individuals, visiting activities of youth organisatins in other countries). The basic communication between young environmentalists and the direct confrontation with experiences from different countries is vital for international co-operation on environmental issues. Especially in countries where formal co-operation between youth environmental organisations is through highly integrative levels, such as the Youth Unions in socialist countries, this grass roots activity has contributed much to the success of the international youth environmental movement.

GREENWAY - AN EMERGING YOUTH ENVIRONMENTAL NETWORK IN SOCIALIST EUROPE

A lot of international nature expeditions have been held in Socialist Europe since the 1960s, by students from environmental university groups and environmental committees attached to socialist student or youth unions. In Hungary, in 1985, a meeting took place which directly involved these groups. The participants, from Hungary, Poland, Czechoslovakia and Romania, developed a scheme for more regular co-operation on a local and international level.

The participants at the meeting represented quite diverse organisations and institutions. Presentations were made to familiarise each other with activities, successes and problems. In this way, each participant gained a better overview of the organisations in his or her own country and in other Socialist countries.

Environmental activities among youth and students in Socialist Europe have spread rapidly in the 1980-85 period. Local groups are unfortunately not much informed about each other's existence and working methods. So it is evident that a scheme for a network of regular co-operation is needed. It was decided to use the name 'Greenway'.

As the final release says:

> We also agreed that official environmental policy has to be improved (...) For increasing the efficiency of our work, we found it necessary to join already existing networks (...) We found it necessary to strive to agree for both exchange of information and people (...) Because of the specific common issues in Socialist countries, we decided to organise our own network. We searched for possibilities to include the other Socialist countries (GDR, USSR, Bulgaria and Yugoslavia) by contacting national youth organisations.

INTERNATIONAL YOUTH ENVIRONMENTAL ACTIONS

Youth environmental organisations are involved in the entire spectrum of environmental action. Sometimes international youth actions are carried out to protect the natural and human environment, often with an educational focus. Often ideas for international youth actions arose at regular camps. Camps for nature studies and protection were organised in farms, in communities of fishermen, around touristic centres and even close to industrial areas. These brought young people into contact with very different views and convinced them that nature protection on a long-lasting basis is only to be achieved through building support for conservation in local communities, among resource users, with the help of tourists and the greater community and last, but not least, by political action through the establishment of pressure groups.

Two examples of international youth environmental actions are presented here: boat actions for regional seas and the project on acid rain.

The IYF organised twice an international boat action: in 1980 for the Waddenzee and in 1983 for the Baltic Sea. They might be called 'public education campaigns'. However, the preparations and also the action itself, had additionally an enormous value for the education of young people on controversial environmental issues. Participants in the actions, local activists who co-operated, and through them youth environmental organisations as a whole had an enormous learning experience.

THE WADDENZEE BOAT ACTION 1980

The ideas for a Waddenzee Boat action germinated in 1979, with the IYF Waddenzee Project. Coincidentally, the plan for an environmental cruise on the Rhine materialised almost simultaneously. Thus, two major public awareness campaigns, similar in form and spirit, each on a vital environmental issue of European concern, were scheduled for summer 1980.
The following aims were laid down:

1. To create and stimulate public awareness of the outstanding ecological values and numerous environmental problems in the Waddenzee region, with special attention to the international dimension.

2. To put pressure on the governments of the Netherlands, the Federal Republic of Germany and Denmark, to take conservation measures and establish the necessary international co-operation.

The Action was particularly aimed at a constructive dialogue with tourists and, most of all, the local population, which has a decisive role in building the political will necessary to conserve the Waddenzee. A natural target for a youth group was young people living in the Waddenzee area whose awareness will be of crucial importance in the long run. Finally, it was hoped that the Action would help to bring together the numerous local and regional conservation groups in the Waddenzee area. The Action involved as much as possible local environmental groups in the preparation and implementation of the activities.
The Boat Action covered three weeks. The cargo clipper *Avontuur* sailed from Rotterdam (Netherlands) to Esbjerg (Denmark). Besides information booths, street theatre, press conferences, public fora, a mobile exhibition, etc. in many places special actions were carried out, focussed on the local situation. In Rotterdam, empty bottles were sold to the public including postcards addressed to the Minister of Environmental Affairs, protesting against the adverse effects of Rhine pollution on the Waddenzee. In the Federal Republic of Germany, the co-operation with fishermen was very effective. Fishing boats sailed with the clipper, making the entrance into a harbour even more attractive. They displayed their morning's catch on the quay

and the pollution-deformed fish deeply impressed the passers-by.

Lectures are not always the most effective method, although indispensable. A simulation drama of an oil spill was carried out in Wilhelmshaven and Cuxhaven, important ports for tankers. People dressed in white protective clothing rushed around, handing out leaflets to the astonished people. The leaflets announced the sudden occurrence of a major oil spill nearby and listed emergency safety precautions. On the reverse side of the leaflets, it was explained why the oil catastrophe was faked. People were clearly unaware of the actual risk.

In Denmark, a two-day festival was arranged, along with the usual programme of public awareness activities. Because of an action near a controversial dyke, there was a heated discussion in the Danish press.

THE BALTIC SEA BOAT ACTION 1983

The idea for this action came up at an IYF training course in Poland in 1981. Two years were needed to work out a joint campaign of youth environmental organisations in the Baltic states. In 1982, many summer camps enabled young environmentalists to dive deeply into Baltic issues, to build up personal experience, to find the best ways to run the campaign, to prepare materials, etc. A special bi-monthly magazine was set up, which has been instrumental in coordinating a large group of people. 'Baltic Sea Books' and background information were produced continuously.

Five boats with representatives of youth environmental organisations took part in the Baltic Sea Boat Action: one each from the FRG, Denmark, Sweden, Poland and Finland. The boats moored in many harbours, where a varied programme was carried out for inhabitants and tourists, including lectures, information stands, beach excursions, street theatres, slide shows, films, panel discussions, drawing actions, music programmes, etc.

Four of the five boats met in Stockholm. The boat from Poland had Polish permission to sail to Stockholm, but did not get Swedish permission to enter Sweden. In Stockholm, an international symposium was held, concentrating on the pollution of the Baltic. The symposium finished with a large debate on 'the Future of the Baltic'.

THE IYF PROJECT ON ACID RAIN

In the early seventies, several Swedish scientists announced serious acidification of lakes in their country, as a result of sulphuric air pollution by heavy industries in middle Europe. At that time, the international community hardly perceived this as a problem. In 1976, 'Natur og Ungdom' (Nature and Youth - Norway) saw that it was very urgent to raise awareness about the serious effects of acid rain. They organised a meeting with youth environmental organisations from the United Kingdom and the Federal Republic of Germany, to start an international project on Acid Rain. Starting a new project also meant developing many different new activities. Activities were necessary to show ecological principles to young people by informative posters in universities and schools, to emphasise the importance of international environmental protection and to bring all this to a broader public by means of leaflets, posters and many outdoor actions.

In the beginning, the project was mainly a 'solidarity' project with the Scandinavian people and environment.

In the summer of 1977, in the main (pedestrian) shopping street of Hamburg (FRG), the first street action against acid rain with international participants took place. 5000 leaflets were distributed which after a few hours proved to be not enough to meet the actual demand. Participants were involved in explanations as well as street theatre or self-composed songs about acid precipitations using traditional melodies. Because an international training course was just finished in Denmark, 40 people from many countries could participate.

Passers-by could compare intact and acidified fresh water ecosystems in aquaria. Long discussions took place on how smog from Germany industries could destroy fresh water ecosystems in Scandinavia.

In the years following, local youth environmental groups started to inform their members and communities about the dangerous effects of air pollution. The international actions were always followed up by numerous activities at national and local level, which again regularly generated international actions by stimulating young people to do something. Discussion and education were carried out at all levels. As there was at that time not much scientific material about ecological aspects of acidification, many groups made their own publications, slide shows, etc. IYF brought out a special issue of its magazine, which contained useful information.

Rather successful postcard actions were carried out regularly, e.g. one in 1979 to the governments of the UK, GDR and FRG. Postcard actions have two aims. One is to influence decision-makers. The other is to create awareness in large parts of the population using a very compact text. Postcards make many people think about the problem and consider their position and enable them to do something, just by signing the postcard.

A new push to the project was given after an IYF intercamp in Sweden in 1982. A group of 25 young Europeans met for 10 days to learn, see and discuss about acidification. At the camp, the idea for an international acid rain week was born.

In April 1983, the first 'International Acid Rain Week' took place. One purpose was to bring the acidification topic to the local groups of youth organisations, and to carry out activities on acid precipitation in a less centralised way. Working groups in several youth environmental organisations (especially in Sweden, FRG, the Netherlands and Belgium) had started working on the topic and had carried out multiple activities in their countries (seminars, excursions, publications, etc.). Another goal of the week was to create large-scale publicity and indirectly to influence the responsible decision-makers, through a massive action of IYF member organisations and other environmental organisations (Greenpeace, Friends of the Earth).

During the week, many public actions were carried out at many places. The week was a trial for such a decentralised action, but turned out to be very successful. The International Acid Rain Week became a regular annual event.

In the summer of 1983, an IYF training course was organised in the Black Forest (FRG), covering the scientific and political background of acid rain, field investigations as well as street actions in Freiburg and Strasbourg. Particular attention was focussed on the death rate of trees in Central Europe and on theoretical and practical training. Two days of the course were spent in street actions.

The acid rain topic finally got a public breakthrough in 1984. There is all the more reason to believe that the campaigning of European youth environmental organisations has activated people in the entire environmental movement to act together against acidification. Especially the creation of the International Acid Rain Week made the theme a popular item for environmental groups. It also made the subject accessible for the media and the general public.

IYF made many more sensational actions. For example, in 1984 three boys and three girls of the German Youth League for Nature Studies (FRG) requested the Embassy of Sweden in the Netherlands for ecological asylum in Sweden. The reason given was that the FRG government did not keep its word. The newly built Buschhaus electricity plant was permitted to run until 1987 without any desulphurication installation.

However, the catalysing role of youth environmental groups in the field of acidification is more or less over now; the issue is taken over by professional groups. At present, youth environmental organisations are creating new fields of action, to use the knowledge and experiences of these ten years.

IYF Europe was one of the initiators of an all-European forest action in 1986-87. The so-called 'European Youth Forest Action' focusses on the destruction of the last untouched forests in Europe, irresponsible forest management, erosion problems, forest death by acidification and European connections with deforestation in the Third World. The Action is a platform of youth groups from all over Europe including, besides the youth environmental organisations, many youth organisations in other fields.

OBSTACLES AND SUCCESSES

Team-working on the environment, as in the cases presented here, encounters many difficulties. It is obvious that practical shortcomings are prominent, since continuously new inexperienced people are involved, e.g. announcements for meetings are badly printed or sent too late, external contacts have to be re-established continuously, information systems are not always well kept, funding applications are not written well or are forgotten until too late. Altogether, the atmosphere is often like some desperate effort to save a sinking ship.

However, all this is also a strength and closely related to the philosophy of open learning through team-working. Every detail of the job is dependent on activities of volunteers. Whether it is a community action, a youth leader training course, a boat campaign or another international project, each aspect is organised and supported by many people. Because of this bottom-up way of working, concrete initiatives are supported, basic needs are filled and many people learn.

Because only involved people are active, not all youth will be attracted to this way of working. The self-governing youth movements are composed of voluntary people who like to find their own way to carry out their idealism themselves. These movements will always stay rather small and involve only a fraction of youth. On the other hand, people who are interested find the right atmosphere to develop themselves into leaders.

As at local and national level, international youth co-operation is also characterised by active democracy. This means that the central co-ordination of IYF is formed by enthusiastic volunteers. A problem is that these people, although well experienced in a national organisation, have an insufficient overview of the complex world of international institutions. Time is scarce and understanding to work with international agencies needs an introduction period. Therefore, youth organisations tend to instruct their representatives to do 'the more urgent matters' first.

So co-operation with international agencies runs well as long as people find the interest, time and opportunity to do it. People wish to devote their inspiration and time to continue with projects rather than in 'supporting jobs' like fund-raising and reporting. In fact, the biggest obstacle in youth environmental action is its own success. Involvement in youth environmental organisations is for everybody a major and effective educational experience: so effective, that people leave and are lost to the movement.

Moreover, proper international reporting is often hardly considered useful. One reason is that project development, management and execution are highly integrated in all activities, and done by a changing - open - team of people; so many activists are well informed without a report. Another reason is that many people get their information from the small reports or articles which are continuously produced in hundreds of youth bulletins, a slide show by somebody who participated, etc. This information is available in the local languages and can much better be used by local youth environmental groups than reports in English.

A third reason is that results of each activity are more or less immediately implemented in new ideas and new activities. Thus an overall report may be difficult to make since each aspect of a project is continuously adapted to new perceptions. Those starting a youth project have often little ideas where it will end. (Quite a few times in the adult world, as shown by the International Acid Rain Week).

In this way, team-working results in bad reporting. This is exactly one of the reasons why youth environmental action is hardly known by the large media and by the international community, even by expert organisations like UNEP and IUCN.

PERSPECTIVES FOR THE FUTURE

Youth environmental activities produce many people who can apply their knowledge and experiences in various environmental fields. Because participants are engaged deeply during the kinds of activities we have described, international co-operation arises easily with many ramifications. Friendships arise and because many people continue in some way in the environment movement 'in their adult life', the necessary network for international co-operation is built up gradually.

The weaknesses and strengths of open-learning go closely together. One may wonder if it is possible to eliminate the weaknesses and to improve the strengths. Is it possible that the youth environmental movement will achieve its goals better, will improve its efficiency, without undermining its capacity for open-learning?

Elements making for improvement are certainly greater recognition in the outside world, spreading experiences of team-working on environment and offering more services to possible users. There is a lot to say in favour of a better equipped central co-ordination in IYF, with some employed people who can stay involved longer and take care of administration, reporting and some of the external contacts (media, international institutions). All this will mean a wider and more continuous spreading of experience, and thus a larger support and recognition of youth environmental work. The IYF experience could be used much more by governmental and non-governmental organisations at national and international level. Especially with regard to other youth organisations, e.g. those working community development, education and training, it would be very fruitful and appreciated if IYF was enabled to offer more services.

Also to its own member organisations, IYF could supply more information and training facilites. Because the more difficult tasks (funding, promotion) would be taken away from the direct activists, it might be argued that more people would benefit from the framework for open-learning which IYF established.

Nevertheless, the costs of a more professional central co-ordination in IYF may be high: the self-governing youth movement will loose some of its youth by more effectively dealing with international institutions and by a professional running of large scale publicity. The opportunities to acquire skills through desperately trying to do everything with inexperienced people will vanish at least partly. Also the manner in which contacts between youth environmental groups are maintained will change, not always for the better, since some of the personal involvement will be lost.

It is a pity that the status quo of the world is such that youth action is badly understood and partly because of that not recognised. Also the educational effects on young people and in the wider community are difficult to demonstrate. This holds for many forms of democratic learning. A basic professionalisation could improve the situation, but also block some valiant aspects of team-working by youth environmental organisations. It remains a question whether the self-governing youth organisations have to adapt, or whether the adult world, the professional organisations and institutions must develop a more open eye, in order that each other's resources will be used better by all parties.

Chapter Six

NEW ROLES FOR INTERNATIONAL ACTION

S. Briceño and D.C Pitt

The day one of us started work on this paper in a little Swiss mountain village, there was some very sad news. One of the young men of the village, Yvan Levyraz, an electrician in the summer, a ski instructor in the winter, had gone in 1983 to Nicaragua as an expert of the Oeuvre Suisse d'Entre-aide Ouvrière. He had, after a visit, come back to Switzerland and organised a first workers' brigade to go to Nicaragua. Later he had helped train the Nicaraguans for 'auto con- struction' - the process of allowing the local people to direct their own construction projects themselves in the cities. In July 1986, he was shot by the Contras.

Yvan was a very impressive man. He had great patience in teaching children to ski, especially with those who were handicapped. His friends called him *un homme de terre*, a man of the earth. He did not have university training, but had learned from many jobs to be intensely practical. He was a giant in all senses, a big man with a great mane of red hair and a beard. But more than his strength and practicality was his ability to communicate, across all the cultural and social boundaries. He was from all accounts *l'étranger le plus connu et aimé dans la region de Matagalpa*[1] - 'the best known and best loved stranger in Matagalpa' - of the area in Nicaragua where he lived, worked and chose to be buried. And the tears that flowed in the eyes of the people of Matagalpa as they crowded the poor streets of their town to watch the cortège in the hot tropical sun flowed no less in the eyes of his fellow villagers as they too stood in silence before the ritual fire on the First of August (the anniversary of the founding of the Swiss state) as the cold evening wind ran through the mountain forests.

We could not help asking ourselves, cannot one find in the life of Yvan Leyvraz, or in the pantheon of practical folk heroes from William Tell to Ché Guevara, more lessons for life, for development, for the environment, for education than all the dry books and treatises that crowd

111

the shelves of planners and experts? We write this essay in the belief that people like Yvan Leyvraz provide the example for the stuff from which we must construct both the theory and the practice for future societies, societies in which self-reliance, closeness to the earth and fundamental human values, human warmth and communication are the touchstones - societies which abhor the exploitation, the injustice, the violence, the hatreds, the war and militarism which killed Yvan.

The present is a timely moment for reflection and action. Poverty in the South is increasing. There are perhaps 1.5 billion people for whom the basic needs of health, food, shelter, education, do not exist, who live often in situations of environmental degradation, in rural wastelands and city slums. Much of the reason for this sad state is that both the arms race and the literally hundreds of wars, most in countries like Nicaragua, draw off the vitally needed resources, human and material. There is a weariness with war and want and a concern that even if the global power structures cannot easily be changed, ideas can and should. Young people especially look forward to a different future, and want their education to be part of it. Even the intellectuals are coming to reflect this belief.

Historians in the future may look back at the late twentieth century and see in it a watershed in thinking about education. The formal structure of education has come under great attack. Illich and others have talked about de-schooling society so that social inequalities may not be perpetuated. But other forces for other reasons may have de-schooled society already and mainly because of social inequalities. In the developing countries of the South universal primary education had hardly been accepted as an ideal before most children were absent or dropped out mainly because they were forced into child labour by great increases in poverty. In the West education, particularly higher education, was attacked especially by the right wing politicians in an effort to reduce public spending in societies where wealth differentials were increasing.

The decline of education in the West, however, may possibly be explained by more fundamental social phenomena. Aries[2] has divided recent history into periods when children or other age groups were the focus of attention and resources. For many years the child was the centre but by the end of the twentieth century the child had become something of an endangered species. A contraceptive

112

technology and a ubiquitous materialism in combination reduced or extinguished the family in both North and South and made schools and teachers redundant. A grey revolution commenced as longevity was no longer a rarity. Youth and women of reproductive age were suspect, increasingly excluded from the power structure and the knowledge that was required to be part of it. Many of those who took part in continuing education (as in the Universities of the Third Age) were part of the geriatric class, though the experience of the old is very important. The younger people were often unemployed, learning therefore nothing on the job, confined to a philistine and inactive subculture of TV, pop and increasingly drugs. A small, mainly male, elite proceeded through formal reducation structures into well paid jobs where supplements of training and experience moved them further away from the unemployed and indeed from the feminine world, as marriage and reproduction declined.

These elites emerged in all countries however poor, and whatever their origins they came to have common characteristics and even subculture. Much of this is reflected in the education which they planned or in which their children participated. Throughout the South elite education reflected the colonial languages and came to be a means of perpetuating elite status. The export of ideas and institutions from the West was part of a general movement of capital, technology, arms etc, part of a market economy where humanistic values were subservient to the search for short term profit. In general, this exacerbated both poverty and social inequalities. Persuaded to leave subsistence farming to come into cash-cropping or to migrate to the towns to form a reserve army of labour, many people became caught in traps of debt, inflation, interest rates etc. where what they earned or saved could not provide for their basic needs, if indeed they could find employment. Commercialisation, in which short term profits were a dominant motive, had particularly grave environmental effects. Economies of scale meant large scale works, short cuts in safety and pollution standards which endangered health - whilst the largest industry of all, the military, both diverted valuable resources and threatened the whole life system. Nowhere was there an economy of peace.

The education system simply did not provide either materials or media to explain, circumvent or prevent the problems or to provide solutions. The poor people had generally forgotten traditional modes of subsistence, and in some cases, in a syncretic world of old and new, these modes in themselves were obsolete. Many of the elites knew little, and probably cared less, about ways and means of alleviating poverty and environmental degradation.

The tragedy in all this was that never before in human history had so much knowledge been accumulated, and even if ill-digested, it provided some solutions to the major socio-economic and environmental questions, not least from some societies where the emphasis, at some cost to income, has continued to be on education, health, mothers and children. Additionally, the mechanisms for storing and diffusing this information are readily and relatively cheaply available through computerisation, and most significantly there is the radio, now found in the remotest parts. Finally, the conceptual frames, open learning, non-formal education - whatever label was stuck on them - were in place too even if much under-utilised and somewhat ethnocentric.

The purpose of this paper is to suggest some of the guiding principles that might form part of an expanded international programme of education for ecodevelopment, i.e. the combination of environmental and development progress, and to spell out the role that organisations like IUCN might play in the future.

Our intention is not however to reinvent the wheel; much has been done by international agencies, notably UNESCO and IUCN which was a child of that postwar euphoria in Paris. Environmental education in the IUCN goes back to the Constitutive Act of the Union signed in Fontainebleau on October 1948 which determined that the Union should promote and recommend 'national and international activities relating to an extensive programme of education, the spread of public knowledge, the collection, analysis, interpretation and dissemination of information'. The Commission on Education was the first Commission to be formed (1949) and immediately took action to ensure that establishment at all levels. It remained for some years the only Commission to be active.

After a relatively quite period in the fifties and early sixties there was a new international momentum in the late 1960s, encouraged by IUCN and CEduc. At a symposium on environmental education in Switzerland in 1960, general principles were set out. In 1970 there was an important IUCN meeting in Nevada which paved the way for major inter-governmental meetings in Belgrade (1975) and Tbilisi (1977). In Nevada a definition was proposed which remains the most used:

> Environmental education is the process of recog-
> nising values and clarifying concepts in order to
> develop skills and attitudes necessary to under-
> stand and appreciate the inter-relatedness among
> man, his culture and biophysical surroundings.
> Environmental education also entails practice in
> decision-making and self-formation of a code of
> behaviour about issues concerning environmental
> quality.

There were other significant developments in the
Fifties. In 1956, IYF (the International Youth Federation of
Environmental Studies and Conservation) was founded as the
youth wing of the IUCN with a dominant interest in education. Though originally based in Europe, IYF's activities are
now located in 45 countries. We have now a great opportunity to share with IYF the implementation of a programme for training youth to become community leaders
around the world.

By the Seventies, notably at the UN Conference on the
Environment (Stockholm 1972), education had come to be
seen as the centre point of a conservation movement which
has adopted a long-term strategic approach to promoting a
holistic ecodevelopment. In 1974 the International
Environmental Education Programme was established by
UNESCO and UNEP. The first formal statement on environmental education, listing aims, objectives, key concepts and
guiding principles, was formulated by experts in the
Belgrade Charter of 1975. Very wide recommendations were
proposed at the first Intergovernmental Conference on
Environmental Education in Tbilisi in 1976.

By 1980 the World Conservation Strategy had set out
more and specific goals and objectives stressing the need for
a sustainable development, principles that guide all IUCN's
work, including education, training and awareness which had
become Programme Area IV by the time of the last General
Assembly in Madrid in 1984. The achievement of Madrid was
to focus on priorities that were both feasible and fundamental (training, reaching decision-makers, improved
management and natural resources, wider dissemination of
the principles ...).

Although the Stockholm, Belgrade and Tbilisi
Declarations etc., and the World Conservation Strategy

were necessary statements when they were articulated, they still need further development and fine tuning as well as systematic dissemination especially <u>if there is to be a transformation of educational systems to support sustainable development</u>. Difficulties still arise in implementing most if not all of the various strategies recommended. For IUCN's educational purposes, we have identified four specific problems that we suggest should be tackled and are presently being considered by the Commission on Education.

<u>First</u>, a major obstacle has been the <u>weakness of environmental institutions to be effective in promoting and implementing change</u> and particularly in bringing together different sectors of society (government, community, business, academic, etc.) to act in partnership. Needs here are to strengthen leadership and management capacities of decision-makers, especially in government, through training programmes in centres of excellence and also to develop a network with a basic group of training centres for implementing any programmes.

A <u>second</u> has been the <u>slowness of communities to move forward towards self-reliant solutions</u>. At the grass roots there is much knowledge, some of it traditional and indigenous, most of it relevant to promoting the alternative, self-reliant way towards sustainable development, but still not systematically used and integrated into global and long term educational processes. Transforming such materials into 'sustainable educational change' requires much action and investment in continuing and systematic programmes. Needs here are to strengthen community organisations, especially NGOs, for self-reliance, through training of youth leaders, and plans for developing environmental education resource centres in botanic gardens, zoos, museums and schools.

<u>Third</u>, regarding <u>training</u> in general there are the following problems:

1. Too specialised and narrow with too little on sustainable development and global interconnections.

2. Too technical/scientific with weak emphasis on managerial/organisational skills improvement.

3. Too remote from real institutions and community processes.

116

4.   Too top-down with too little attention to the grass roots, the cultural contexts, or traditional knowledge.

5.   Too little into information and communication systems.

Fourth, there is an easing in momentum at the international level just at a time when national demands multiply and local enthusiasm quickens. There is particularly an insufficiency in international efforts to assist in the transfer of information and in training, an activity which the ILO has called a basic need to be put alongside food, health, shelter, etc. The need here is to strengthen IUCN's information capacity to transfer and exchange useful data related to training and educational opportunities. Regarding the international level, there is also need to promote environmental ethics and transform educational systems to promote sustainable development.

But we might ask whether all this is enough and if such a programme will succeed in solving the great ecodevelopment problems faced in the modern world. Perhaps some additional elements are needed. At present, it is estimated that as many as 1.5 billion people have their basic needs unfulfilled and many live in degraded, fragile or threatened ecosystems. In general, these very poor people are either illiterate, or do not have sufficient knowledge and information to promote their own welfare, or to participate effectively in the wider social, economic and political structure. UNESCO has made some estimates that only one child in three of school age in developing countries (5-15 years) is in fact in school. Many (perhaps 250 million) are working especially in exploitative urban settings. Another group, perhaps again 250 million, are what are described as unemployed. Both these groups, even if they become or were once literate, have very few skills, and also since they are most often to be found in an urban environment have few opportunities to draw on any traditional knowledge of environmental matters. What all this means is that the group of very poor and illiterate people is likely to grow in the future as the present young generation grow up. We suggest that reaching this group with an appropriate education is the prime challenge and may need a major strategy in its own right.

What is involved? Several points should be noted. First, the 1.5 billion we are talking about are not all, not mainly completely destitute and dying. Admittedly many have tropical diseases of one kind or another, but these conditions, whilst reducing daily effectiveness, do not necessarily affect longevity or the ability to participate in education. More important, these people are only illiterate in the sense of having an unfamiliarity with written languages. They have often an incredibly complex oral culture with often much more sophistication in categorising parts of the environment than Western cultures. Cold environment people, such as Eskimos for example, may have 50 or more words for snow. Tropical forest people, such as Amazonian Indians, have great ethnobotanical knowledge. All this reflects the very detailed knowledge and intimacy these people have with their environment.

Secondly, there is an intense desire for relevant knowledge. In the colonial period, in many countries where schools were opened, they were inundated with students and applicants. In recent years, so many students have graduated that some could speak of a Diploma Disease. The problem has rather been the disillusion that people have found with an education that is not relevant. But more significantly social change, especially the commercialisation of daily activities, has made traditional knowledge largely irrelevant. The purpose of the introduced education was often seen to be to provide people with skills which could lead to earning a living. But in the cash economy there were too few jobs and often the education itself was too general and provided inappropriate skills. The situation was then one in which people had no education, traditional or modern. In many environmentally degraded areas an important cause of neglect and exploitation can be traced to this vacuum. The decline of the taboo system for example may be a most important reason for species loss, especially where it is associated with short term outside commercial exploitation.

Thirdly, there is currently a situation where there is a great pool of knowledge about sustainable development and environmental management. This is partly the product of scientific research but also a legacy of traditional materials that have been collected by anthropologists and others.

Fourthly, there are readily available media by which knowledge can be transferred or retrieved. We live in the midst of a telecommunications and computer revolution which thrives in an oral rather than a written culture. There are, for example, audiotheques in Mali where people record traditional secrets of environmental grass roots management on cassettes. There are data bases from which people can demand environmental information, rather like the medical 'husky', a mini computer which will give a diagnosis from symptoms presented. Most of all there is the ubiquitous radio, especially talkback radio where there can be debate and dialogue, as well as the telephone which ITU wants to put in every village within the next few years.

Given this situation what additional strategies might we add to those already proposed? We might suggest an open learning programme, possibly building on existing distance teaching, radio schools etc. The hardware exists and the institutional mechanisms, what is lacking is the input - relevant syllabi that would cover conservation and development not from a public awareness point of view but with special emphasis on the self-reliant needs and wants of people at the grass roots. The emphasis therefore might be appropriate technology, guidelines on how to use available services as well as rehabilitated traditional and indigenous knowledge materials. More ambitiously, ways might be found of having major data bases nationally including an audiotheque element where ordinary people could obtain oral as well as written materials on demand.

Perhaps all of this is still rather a little too top-down. If people only learn from what is made available to them, the difference from centralised pedagogical practices may not be great. There is not de-schooling, to use Illich's terminology. Ways perhaps should be sought of permitting local people at the grass roots to put their own ideas in through dialogues. This process however may only be communication amongst elites, especially if any dialogue takes place in the informational sphere where the colonial languages and mores still predominate. This, of course, is still useful but not necessarily helpful to the most deprived groups, the so-called Fourth World, the very poor - outcaste peoples, subproletariats, as well as other disadvantaged groups such as women, young people, disabled people, etc. In the past others have spoken for them, or having been deprived by colonialism of their own personae, they may tend to emulate the colonial images in what Paulo Freire has called the 'culture of the oppressed'. Conservationists have talked about the necessity of environmental rehabilitation. This may mean new roles, a process of participant research, for example where the real problems of the Fourth World can be discovered from close encounters. A dialogue with the deprived will be a most difficult process, not least because governments do not often want to admit inequalities of this kind in their own midst. The spin-off from improving the lot of the most deprived through educative processes will be enormous since these poorest people often live in threatened and fragile environments and their poverty itself is the result of a vicious circle in which environmental degradation plays a major part.

The IUCN, especially through its Commission on Education, as it represents governments as well as non-governmental organisations, may be a productive forum for promoting and exchanging the kinds of ideas we have proposed here.

NOTES

1   Vingt Quatre Heures, Lausanne 30 juillet 1986
2   Aries, P., 1960, L'enfant et la vie familiae, Plonn, Paris
3   Illich, I., 1973, De-Schooling Society, Penguin, Harmondsworth.
    Defence for Children, Geneva.

PART TWO

THIRD WORLD SITUATIONS

Chapter Seven

THE EMERGING CONSERVATION MYSTIQUE IN THE DOMINICAN REPUBLIC

Sophie Jakowska

In the triumphant age of science and technology, environmentalists are finally willing to admit that science is a product of people, with all their failings and prejudices, and it is not value free. Some may say that science and technology have failed environmental education by offering an illusion that they can solve all the environmental problems they cause.

Now, on the international level, ethical religious insights are being recognised as probably the single most important resource for humanity in the desperate struggle to restore the balance to our plundered planet. On the local level, in the Dominican Republic, there seems to emerge these days a clear recognition that it is not sufficient to have economic incentives to pull the country out of the precarious situation. Work mystique and traditional austere values are being invoked together with ethical and patriotic incentives[1].

Such patriotic motivation for the protection of natural resources has been inserted in children's books[2,3,4] with the hope that these ideas shall reach teachers, parents and other adult co-readers. This approach was presented to teachers at a workshop on children's literature[5], showing how to use these texts to make children understand that natural resources are really part of the national heritage, and deserve the same respect as the monuments and the symbols of the fatherland.

Independently, a new kind of concern for nature, and for the forests in particular, is revealing itself today in the Dominican Republic. It seems to be the product of multiple projects in conservation and human development, undertaken with different approaches by individuals and organised groups. Some of these originate as grass roots movements, others are related to private or government institutions, and some are sponsored by international agencies.

It is interesting that most of the people involved are

not only concerned with the eco-socio-economic aspects of conservations, but are aiming at creating a conservation awareness that appeals to the sentiments rooted in the patriotic and religious convictions of the participants.

The appearance of the new IUCN-inspired conservation for development clubs named LAURELES within this emerging conservation climate is very timely, since the clubs are promoting a similar conservation mystique of their own.

In keeping with its social doctrine, the Roman Catholic Church provides religious orientation in favour of conservation and of the proper use of the natural resources so that they may be shared by all. In the Dominican Republic there are numerous well-documented examples of ecologically positive initiative and action that originated within the Church or in Church-related groups[6]. Other Christian and inter-denominational groups are also increasingly involved in conservation.

Antonio Camilo, a Catholic priest[7], used the coincidence of World Forest Day on 20 March, and a week later of Palm Sunday - in 1983, a year dedicated to Reforestation in the Dominican Republic - to point out that the traditional Palm Sunday procession is a liturgical celebration of the forest. He quoted paragraph No. 139 of the Puebla document[8], in which the faithful of Latin America are warned about the deleterious effects of the irrational exploitation of the natural resources and of environmental pollution, both for people and for the ecological balance.

The Puebla document itself contains a considerable amount of environmental education, which has been analysed in Spanish[9] and English[10]. Camilo further quotes Puebla No. 1236: 'it is an obligation of all Christians and of the Church to preserve natural resources created by God for all people in order to transmit them as an enriched heritage to the future generations.'

The liturgical symbolism of Palm Sunday should motivate all the Christians to respect the life of trees as necessary for human life, and to encourage each Dominican to make a personal commitment to the national flora.

In the same year, 1983, a major Catholic youth movement, known as Pascua Juvenil, under the general theme of 'Reconciliation is Liberation', dedicated p.20-26 to reconciliation with nature[11]. The suggested bibilical readings included Genesis 1; Romans 8, 18-28, and 2 Thess. 3, 7-12. Analysis of Genesis was made in terms of a text called 'Anti-Genesis', in which man sets himself as creator of things, in an inverted order, and finally as creator of God himself in his human image, and with disastrous effects.

In this same brochure[11], which is used for study and discussions, the recommended readings include Puebla No. 492 and *Gaudium et Spes* No. 34, the latter a document from Vatican II. The texts are to be considered in relation to the community in which the young people live.

Emphasis is also made on human work as a form of reconciliation with nature in terms of the encyclical *Laborem Exercens*[12]. The selection for group singing is a song of Nelson Ned extolling the merits of the rural worker.

In January 1984 an entire rural community of San José de Ocoa, under the leadership of a Canadian priest, José Luis Quinn, met on nine consecutive evenings for Masses at which they prayed for the environment. It was an impressive display of ecologically oriented liturgy and homilies delivered by the clergy and by lay persons. There was an obvious sincere participation on the part of the faithful and at offertory time little trees were brought to the altar.

Without going into the details of some pastoral letters of the Dominican bishops which deal with the environment, listed[13] and discussed[6] elsewhere, it is proper to call attention to the fact that even in the turbulent pre-election period the Episcopal Conference issued on 3 May 1986 an extensive document telling the candidates for office what it means to serve in the government in the light of the Roman Catholic teaching. One part refers to the obligation of the government to protect natural resources from the merciless attacks of irrational human egoism. According to God's plan, man must be a faithful steward and a diligent caretaker of nature - soil, rivers, coasts, atmosphere, plants, trees and animals - and never a systematic and irresponsible aggressor and destroyer[14].

Earlier, in February 1986, the officers of the Instituto Dominicano de Bio-Conservacion, a grass roots organisation, asked the candidates for the presidency to define their position on a number of environmental issues[15]. As far as I know, there was no publicity giving their answers.

Independently, a proposal was made to establish in the future government a Ministry or Institute of Forests and Waters[16], which may be overlooking some of the existing institutions which, with some incentive, could certainly perform very well.

As 1986 Arbor Day approached, the statements in the press referring to deforestation rose to a more emotional pitch, citing the facts from the FAO 1985 document which shows that the Dominican Republic is the fifth on the list of the most forest-depleted countries of the Americas. Articles called for the right of every Dominican to live at peace with nature and for establishing a national environmental policy[17]. Irreversible desertification was presented as an imminent danger in view of the ecological catastrophe in the neighbouring Republic of Haiti. 'Environmental illiteracy' of the Dominicans was cited as a serious impediment for a rational action on the part of the professionals.

Editorials on deforestation described it as the first and most important problem of physical nature[18] and as a tragedy[19]. The latter alludes to the moving speech delivered by Enrique Armenteros Ruis, of Progressio Foundation, on the occasion of the publication of a book by the former director of the national parks, Merilio Morell[20].

As Morell stated on the same occasion[21]: the destruction of the forests cannot be blamed exclusively on 'bad' villagers, or on 'bad' businessmen, but on the fact that what has been done was not prohibited by law, or that the laws that prohibited it could not be enforced. Social injustice simply obliged people to destroy the forests in order to survive.

The lack of concern for the environmental problems and for conservation is due principally to the fact that the majority of people cannot share in the cultural phenomena of their species because they have no material or spiritual means for the full exercise of their human condition. Their individual and collective resources are being wasted away in the daily struggle for survival[22].

In anti-conservation acts economic interests prevail in most cases. Certainly, there seems to be a need for a single code of morals applicable to private and public life. For the believers, the ultimate for knowing right from wrong is God's law. More people who consider themselves in God's service are becoming involved in conservation harmonious with human development in the belief that 'Victory will go to the one who bests reflects God's plan', in the words of Monsignor Oscar Romero, martyr bishop of El Salvador. Such people take a stand against deforestation, denouncing the abuses[23].

The most recent statement by a Catholic bishop on the subject of reforestation is that by Juan Antonio Flores Santana of the Diocese of La Vega. In a circular dated 4 May 1986[24] he brings up the courageous stand against deforestation by Carlos Guerra Perez-Carral, from Cevicos, whose suggestions he lists for other members of the diocesan clergy; among others, a great participation of the Church in raising public awareness on the forest problem and in promoting a patriotic-religious mystique of reafforestation. The issue was present as a matter of life and death for the country. A meeting of Catholic clergy and other persons interested in reafforestation was held on 13 May near la Vega, in Ponton, chaired by Monsignor Roque Adames, founder of the internationally famous Plan Sierra.

It is significant that on Arbor Day, 5 May 1986, one of the recipients of the medal awarded by the Comision Nacional Técnica Forestal for reafforestation work is a Catholic priest, Fr. Luis Quinn, from the ecologically-minded community of San José de Ocoa[25].

It is strange, on the other hand, that in this island nation there seem to be no major protests against the equally serious destruction of the mangroves, which fall victim to the supposedly correct 'tourist development projects' that would actually benefit from the presence of mangroves for aesthetic reasons. Besides these are habitats of ecological and economic importance. Data published in the April-June 1984 IUCN Bulletin were brought to public attention by Antonio Thomen, an active conservationist[26].

As a matter of fact, mangroves, like the coral reefs, are protecting the coastline and their destruction is followed by a gradual loss of soil at the fringe of erosion. Thus, those who destroy mangroves (and reefs) are indirectly responsible for subtraction of national wealth by diminishing the national territory.

Ramon Leonardo, a Christian singer dedicated to the apostolate through the arts and communication media, in his weekly article, while talking of peace, added: 'Today we are making war against the flora, we cut down forests, we dry out rivers, we shake the tectonic structure, and we contaminate the environment; downright pollution makes the peace tremble ... we live in a constant war against the environment'[27].

Why, then, do we need an International Year dedicated to Peace? Another frustrating experience for the young?

Perhaps we must begin to speak in harsher terms. Nature has been sacrificed at the altar of development and progress. Nature destruction subtracts from national wealth. It must be viewed as a crime comparable to treason and punishable by law.

As is the case with any doctrine that is meant to be practiced, the conservationist ideals can only be valued through daily contact and example given by individuals during the activities that are not collectively controlled. The success of environmental ethics (and/or environmental education) depends not on those who preach it (or teach it) but on those who have the courage, perseverance, and strength of convictions to practice it.

Today's youth needs a better understanding of three concepts that are indispensable to ecological balance and to human survival. These are: stewardship, enlightened and responsible; relationship born out of recognition of being 'a very special form of life', but last to appear on this planet; and justice, something that the young are unable to visualise in the context of their own lives.

In the Dominican Republic there is a definite moral crisis which affects youth[28]. Some adopt the ways of consumerism, armamentism, and professionalism based on competition as a way to acquire wealth. They prefer to accept disorder at the national and international level, and injustice, as something normal, a product of the non-participation and inactivity of those who are most needy. Other youths become indifferent or pessimistic, when confronted with life and its possibilities. They see no solution to world's problems and seek refuge in hedonism. If they do work, it is to have money, to enjoy it, to drink liquor or to take drugs. They even find out that it is not necessary to work; one can always manage as long as one stays alive.

The basic education ought to start within the family, but the Dominican family lacks many of the fundamental aspects of the Western society. It is rather a group relationship, in which the children of different fathers and mothers share the same roof and call each other brother or sister. A morally strong father figure is most often absent or, when present in a home, he may be only the 'macho' figure that traumatises both the male and the female descendants. His role may be limited to satisfying some of the material needs of food, shelter and clothing. The mother figure helps perpetuate the 'machismo' by accepting it as normal, and developing it in the sons through preferential treatment of their needs, and considering offspring as a form of economic security for old age.

On the other hand, some young people have discovered their ideals. They start to fight for a new society, with brotherhood and justice. They realise that social wounds may be healed, converting swords into ploughshares, and the human race into a big family. They accept a commitment for peace, with positive action that rejects violence and uses universal love as a reference point. Perhaps school today fails the youth, perpetuating consumerism, competition and conformism, and educating in a mechanical way of knowledge acquisition. Thus the young who seek on their own the path that leads to peace through love must find it outside the home and outside the school. They seek out clubs and other organisations that offer non-formal education and recreation through sports and other healthy activities.

In the Dominican Republic the new conservation for development clubs called LAURELES[29] have a mystique that starts with the laurel from which they take the name LAURELES, and the acrostic derived therefrom, which includes the ideals of work, friendship, unity, responsibility, efficiency, leadership, hope and service.

They are taught to identify with their country's motto: God, Country, Liberty, and are committed to the defence of their country's natural heritage. They are told that one must be sincere and respectful, that trees are meant to be planted, loved and protected for the proper use, and that for each tree that one must cut, ten trees must be planted. This shall make their country beautiful and green.

Youth in the Dominican Republic cannot help observing a large number of people who aspire to leadership without considering that it represents work and a vocation of service to others. Into this society LAURELES try to bring the concept of leadership as work and service. They place great emphasis on their own effort and on mutual help, and on moderation in the use of natural resources. They are involved in caring for trees in nurseries, and building country roads, tubular wells, latrines, cement floors for dwellings and economic stoves, rabbit farming, or surveying the community in order to identify major problems.

LAURELES surround all these activities with the aura of dignity of a high vocation for a purpose that is a better country in accordance with God's plan. They endow their actions with enhanced value and profound meaning and use a simple but moving ritual, which is emotionally enriching. But the ethical and religious basis of the LAURELES movement must be strengthened through an established programme of civics, religion and environmental ethics, to be included on the agenda of every meeting and also as special training courses. For spiritual guidance LAURELES depend on the Youth Ministry of the Archdiocese of Santo Domingo but the way in which this guidance may be best applied has not been established yet.

Young people in the smallest communities realise their potential for social change, but they resent being remembered only at election time. The custom of assigning a theme on national or international level to each year, meant to focus the attention upon an issue for positive and fruitful action, is also a frequent source of frustration. They can remember how the 'Year of the Child' failed to fulfil their expectations in 1979. Similarly, the 'Year of the Forest', the 'Year of the Youth'. Now the 'Year of Peace'?

The natural impatience of youth has to be channelled to avoid such frustrations. In terms of social change a calendar year is relatively insignificant and so little seems to be accomplished on each annual occasion. Yet an instant may be sufficient to affect an individual and to accomplish a transformation which, when multiplied, becomes an effective instrument of progress.

Youth movements are best when they help people achieve a personal change which reflects immediately upon the surroundings. Co-operation is best where there is love and concern for others and for things that belong to all and must be shared fairly by all. No amount of technical or scientific knowledge shall bring about a change in the selfish and the greedy, and stop them from perpetrating ecological crimes for personal benefit. But social censure and good example are most effective in dealing with socially negative elements. Unfortunately, some societies seem to reward crime and vice has a pleasurable connotation, but there is hope in the surging youth movements such as Pascua Juvenil, evangelical choirs, organisations of rehabilitated drug addicts, sports clubs and cultural clubs, where the young people express their opposition to the anti-culture which the false society is trying to impose.

LAURELES place themselves at the service of combating the anti-culture trends in their country using, among others, artistic creativity as an expression of their deep convictions and as a form of recreational education for the entire community.

Members have already produced typical verses (décimas) extolling reforestation efforts, the love of trees and nature, etc. As a result of their founder's teaching, the first LAURELES club in Los Hidalgos produced a folkloric comedy which deals with: (1) deforestation caused by villagers who cut trees to make charcoal; (2) the exodus of the unskilled villagers to the city and; (3) the danger of drugs that the rural Dominican youth are facing at this time. The comedy provides entertainment and education to the communities which the club visits on the occasion of swearing-in of new clubs or for patronal feasts; it has also been recorded on a video cassette.

More reafforestation mystique was included in the programme which was prepared for the first anniversary of LAURELES held on 7 July 1986 in Loma de Cabrera near the Capotillo National Monument. The theatrical performance involved a plot using all the elements of LAURELES ritual and hymn as well as various texts that told of the need to plant trees and what a tree means to the community and to the country. Included were episodes involving a villager first with a machete and later with an axe, threatening the tree which the youngest member had planted and which everyone tried to protect. The act of embracing the tree, introduced in this play, was reminiscent of the 'Chipko' conservation movement of India and intended to bring in the conservation mystique of other cultures.

Symbolic characters such as Mother Earth, the Sun, the Wind, and the Rain, together with the chorus, participate in the dialogue, defending the tree and recriminating the villager who threatens to cut it down. At this moment a messenger arrives with the news about an old mango tree that has been cut down in the colonial part of Santo Domingo. The guilt is thus shared by both the rural and the urban 'tree assassins'. But LAURELES are convincing and gain a new member. The eco-drama ends with a song of Nelson Ned extolling the man who works in the fields.

It is the purpose of this play to provide an emotional didactic experience, stressing the threat of deforestation while offering hope of redemption of nature through love and work and a true reconciliation of man with nature.

Of great importance is the prompt establishment of a continued education programme for LAURELES in order to nurture the patriotic and religious mystique of conservation for development. The study of ecology and conservation, closer to the traditional environmental education, is also an immediate necessity in order to make understandable the actions that are recommended and those that are disapproved. This programme must also address the immediate local problems and emphasise the natural resources as a national heritage, in the case of both resource and non-resource species.

The increasing discovery of the possibilities that nature offers, and learning more about the physical chemical and biochemical phenomena, placing these discoveries at the service of the whole human family, is the way mankind can participate in God's creation[30].

LAURELES must acquire a broad vision of their country's geographic and climatic conditions, habitats that are interesting and unique, species of plants and animals which are the pride of the country and which deserve protection, etc. Agricultural development and other human activities must be seen in the whole environmental picture and supported by the study of IUCN World Conservation Strategy.

Since LAURELES aim at producing better neighbours and better citizens, one ought to offer a programme in human conduct and social etiquette, necessary for individual and group interactions that require decisions and conflict resolution. Civic education must teach the rights and the obligations of the citizens, tell about institutions of the constitutional government, and include a historical content for patriotic enrichment. The study of the social doctrine of the Church shall help to understand the meaning of stewardship of nature which has always been part of Roman Catholic teaching.

Environmental education for LAURELES must include the ethical element (sensitivity and need for self-transcendent values and moral beliefs) and the aesthetic component (the awareness necessary to identify and to demand quality of the environment, also in terms of beauty). But to be holistic, it must also include the practical component[31]. As we overcome the former reluctance to address contents having ethical dimensions, we may search out some of the older principles, traditions and beliefs in order to enrich the framework of the World Conservation Strategy.

The long-term task of environmental education is to foster or reinforce the attitudes and behaviour compatible with the ethical principles[32]. It is also to identify the deficiencies in the public concept of man's relation with the environment that lead to the failure of support by the public of conservation measures. Some characteristics of the educational system may perpetuate those conceptual deficiencies in the general public[33].

World Conservation Strategy provides both the intellectual framework and the practical guidance for the conservation action that is necessary. In material terms it demonstrates that conservation improves the prospects of sustainable development and proposes ways of integrating conservation into the development process. But there must be ways other than those of science and technology, and/or promises of material benefits, for making the choices.

Above all there has to be a recognition of the common good as the principal goal. The common good, in turn, is the sum of those conditions of social life which permit individuals, families and associations to achieve to the best of their capacity their own perfection in physical and spiritual terms[14]. There must be a sincere desire for this common good within the heart of each person.

LAURELES clubs are being formed where youth see few opportunities for progress, where there are no sources of employment, where the use of the existing resources is old-fashioned and inefficient, and where individual and group initiative is minimised by limited perception and lack of knowledge.

But LAURELES represent a liberating experience: a young person becomes exposed to new ways of thinking and of doing things; learns for the first time about a 'club', joint action, planning, decisions, and undertaking projects without waiting for the government to do it; may leave the village perhaps for the first time in life and see other parts of the country; meets strangers, some from more and others from less developed areas; meets people from foreign lands with different customs. For the first time in their lives, the members may face the exaltation of a voluntary contribution to society through work, work which is a privilege and an ennobling act.

To make people 'think with their hearts' in matters of conservation, it is necessary to awaken the sensitivity to minor details, so that, for example, they notice that there seems to be something wrong when a smiling man, in an advertisement, sprays indiscriminately huge and deadly amounts of pesticides, or when couples in love carve their initials on the bark of a centenary tree.

People without sensitivity and without moral convictions cannot carry out ecologically positive plans. LAURELES with their mystique may be able to educate their members in firm moral convictions, preferably based on faith that is practiced in and outside the church.

We cannot predict at this early time the potential of the Conservation for Development Clubs founded upon the patriotic and religious motivations for environmental ethics.

The moment in the Dominican Republic seems propitious in spite of the many social forces that are negative and harmful to youth, because many other groups recognise such values as an indispensable resource or instrument to combat ecological crimes and vices that threaten our lives.

There is an added element, especially for the Dominican people: it is the *patria chica*, the little father-land, or the place where one was born. Among Dominican emigrants the thought of *patria chica* evokes tender feelings. If this *patria chica* becomes known as the place where the ideals of reafforestation and of conservation are preached and put into practice for the common good, such ideals become attractive to Dominicans abroad, and they may donate funds and volunteer work to make their own *patria chica* the most beautiful and ecologically sound habitat of all. LAURELES may become influential in this respect and with their work and attitudes may stimulate support from abroad for local conservation projects.

Their own survival, however, depends on how they preach and practice their conservation gospel. On the whole, LAURELES have a unique opportunity to strengthen the emerging conservation mystique in the Dominican Republic.

NOTES

1. Dobal, Carlos - Mini-articulo; El retorno a los incentivos patrioticos. Listin Diario, 1 May 1986.
2. Jakowska, Sophie. En una isla como la nuestra. Editora Taller. 1978.
3. Jakowska, Sophie. Hijos de la Tierra - Meditaciones para ninos y adultos sobre la proteccion ambiental y la conservacion de recursos. Editora Taller, 1978.
4. Jakowska, Sophie. Amigos del Cocodrilo. Editora Taller. 1979.
5. Jakowska, Sophie. El desarrollo en el nino de actitudes hacia la naturaleza como patrimonio nacional. Seminario-Taller de Literatura Infantil y Juvenil. CILIJ/ONAP/PILI/SEEBAC/BN. June 18-20, 1984.
6. Jakowska, Sophie. 'Roman Catholic teaching and environmental ethics in Latin America.' In: Religion and Environmental Crisis, Eugene Hargrove, editor. University of Georgia Press, 1986 (in print).

7. Camilo, Antonio, Listin Diario, 26 March 1983, p.7.
8. Puebla. La Evangelizacion en el presente y en el futuro de América Latina. CELAM 1979.
9. Jakowska, Sophie. El Documento de Puebla y los Bienes de la Tierra. Circular No. 6. Arzobispado de Santo Domingo, 15 May 1980.
10. Jakowska, Sophie. 'Puebla and the resources of the earth.' In: Ecumenical Packet of Articles Citing Religious Authority Related to Concern for the Environment, CODEL, Inc. Environment and Development Programme. May 1983.
11. Pascua Juvenil. Reconciliacion es Libertacion. 1983.
12. Jakowska, Sophie. '5 Junio 1986: Dia Mundial del Ambiente.' El Camino V(257): 16. 1 June 1986.
13. Jakowska, Sophie. See 10: Roman Catholic Documents with Environmental Implications, and those specific for Latin America and/or the Dominican Republic. May 1983.
14. Pastoral Letter, National Conference of Dominican Bishops, 3 May 1986.
15. 'Los candidatos y la Foresta'. Instituto Dominicano de Bio-Conservacion. Listin Diario, 18 February 1986. p.7.
16. Editorial: 'Un Programita'. Listin Diario, 27 March 1986.
17. Martinez, Eleuterio. 'Necesidad de una politica ambiental.' Listin Diario, 31 December 1985.
18. Editorial, Listin Diario, 17 March 1986.
19. Editorial, Listin Diario, 1 May 1986.
20. 'Armenteros advierte efectos deforestacion.' Listin Diario, 2 May 1986.
21. Morell, Merilio. 'Situacion Forestal en Republica Dominicana.' Listin Diario, 9 May 1986.
22. Jakowska, Sophie. 'Cultura Ambiental.' In: Lecturas para el Dia Mundial del Ambiente, 5 Junio. CIBIMA/UASD 1979.
23. Guerra, Carlos. 'Una accion contra la deforestacion.' Listin Diario, 25 April 1986.
24. Flores Santana, Juan Antonio. Circular 21-IV-86. Obispado de La Vega. El Camino, 4 May 1986.
25. Listin Diario, 3 May 1986.
26. Thomen, Antonio. 'La importancia de los manglares.' El Caribe. Suplemento Agropecuario. 30 January 1986, p.7.
27. Leonardo, Ramon. 'Evangelizando Hoy.' Listin Diario, 21 April 1986, p.6 E.
28. Rosario, Luis. 'La Juventud y la Paz.' Listin Diario, 17

April 1986, p.6.
29. Jakowska, Sophie. 'Conservation for Development Clubs. The Dominican Experience.' Report to CEduc.IUCN. Ottawa, 31 May - 5 June 1986.
30. Synod of Catholic Bishops. Rome, 8 December 1985.
31. Chelliah, Thilla. Ethics and Social Resp. Paper No. 13. Bangalore, 1985.
32. Baes, Albert V. Environment Paper No. 3. Bangalore, 1985.
33. Smyth, John C. Environment Paper No. 2. Bangalore, 1985.

Chapter Eight

THE MIDNIGHT CLASSROOM IN ZIMBABWE

Chris Tobayiwa[1]

If you were barefoot with no jersey and there were no prospects of having either jersey or shoes, and life was such that you had to wake up well before sunrise to go and plough the fields, the idea of a beautiful dawn and golden sunrise seemed irrelevant - and of no consequence. It was more important to develop eyes in the feet. When the morning cold was over and the sun began to blaze it was time to herd cattle, and we were certainly aware of the shade, rather than the bright blue skies of Africa. If the cattle were about to invade the next man's field, there was not time for trying to understand nature. But we learned what it could provide. We could spot wild fruits from afar and we remembered where fruit trees were likely to be found and when the fruits might be ready.

When the rains were upon us, it was not time for poetic inspiration from lightning flashes and the crash of thunder. It was time to put a sack on one's head to protect it from hailstones. It was time to put the cattle into their kraals. To the credit of the adults, they stood by to prevent undue pain. If the rains were too heavy, they took over. Rainbows we did admire, together with the mud and the cool air. Sunset we admired because it was time for change. We could rest by the fire, helping our mothers cook for us.

We did not have an excess of popular foods, but we had plenty of our staple, sadza, with peanut butter and dried vegetables. The relishes varied widely, with fish, beef, goat meat, mutton, game meat, chicken, locusts, mice and other sources of proteins. A variety of green vegetables were available in summer. We supplemented our diet with many wild fruits and milk. In terms of worldly riches there was not that much, but in terms of life we certainly could scream for what we wanted with the hope of getting it - provided our parents were willing.

We learnt from living. We were not trained to be lawyers, or doctors or teachers. One just learnt about being

137

a human being. In this present-day rat race, one may feel that time was being wasted. But morals and wisdom came through stories, usually told by grandparents, and sometimes by parents. The atmosphere was ideal for listening. There was barely sufficient light, beyond the soft glow of the moon, no radio or television, and it was too early to sleep. A circle by the fire was ideal, with grandmother telling stories, her eyes shining as they reflected the flames. And there were games that were played in the dark, such as riddles and other types of guessing games.

Much of our folklore and the fairy tales we listened to with such joy, and sometimes fear, were about life in the wilderness. We were taught the joys and the dangers of doing right and wrong in the wilderness, and we learned to regard it as a treasury of what one needed.

'If you find rotten fruits, do not curse the tree, lest you fail to find your way home,' we were told. 'If you see any creature too small or too ugly, do not gasp or laugh, its creator might be offended.'

Included in the learning process was the art of cropping from the wild. Fruit-bearing trees were generally not used for firewood or anything else - it was *zvaiera*, taboo, to vandalise fruit trees. When we went fishing and we had taken too many worms, we simply re-buried them where they were likely to thrive. If we went hunting and caught one or two animals, we went home secure in the belief that tomorrow we could come again. We could collect honey without destroying the beehive.

Although one learned much about nature in the midnight classrooms, some things had to come later. For us kids, nothing could cause more pandemonium than the existence of a snake anywhere. We used stones, sticks and anything that could wipe out the snake. We used to change our route when snakes were known to live in certain areas. I used to admire an uncle of mine for being a strong and courageous man. But one day I saw him dragging a dead snake, simply to bury it in a ditch, and my whole image of him changed. I had grown up hating snakes so much that I could not be reconciled with anybody who could hold one. It took A-level biology to make me able to forgive my uncle - the biologists taught us about the balance of nature and that snakes were an essential part of the biosystem - but by then my uncle was dead and buried. In spite of all that, my first reaction to a snake is still to get a stick. The learned behaviour is secondary, although now more predominant.

But one snake stood out from the rest; it was the python. This snake stood out on its own in our local culture. It was and still is the totem of the people (Shato). Our bonds with other animals we met in the wilderness were also strengthened by the fact that each of us had a totem animal, and we listened to poems in praise of their elegance, liveliness, dignity and strength. In fact, the totem system meant that we were born into a 'wildlife society'.

School brought its thrills and strangeness. One crazy thing that was hammered into our skulls was to learn how to 'think in English'. That went on throughout primary and secondary school. It might have been fine if we had known how the English thought, or for that matter if the teacher had known how the English thought. It is hard to provide alternative ways in which we could have been taught, but the idea of using fantasy to know how to think in English produced crude results which were neither English nor of any other stable culture. If anything, a cultural inferiority complex developed because suddenly all that we had learnt for the first seven years of our lives was to be discarded as useless.

We learnt the alphabet in song, learnt how to spell in song. We even learnt to speak English in song. Our teacher knew how to reach us. When we started learning about how we were 'discovered' and 'civilised', the songs disappeared. Perhaps the teachers were not good composers, but the inspiration to teach us in song what they did not believe could not come. School was becoming harsh and most of what we learnt was for exams and never fused into the person like the song that moulded opinions.

It was time to go when the sun blazed through the window and the teacher was tired from the strain of handling nearly 45 of us in the class. We would shoot out like mice from a hole, knowing there was freedom when we got back to the most welcome midnight classrooms. There, no one regimented the mind.

I sometimes have the strange feeling that in many ways school was a place to go when your education was already complete. There is that proud feeling that the person had already been made long before the chalk dust had got to our noses. Most of what was relevant to the upkeep of goats, sheep, cattle and chickens had already been instilled in us as far back as one cared to remember. Fishing, hunting and collecting honey were not just hobbies but serious work. We helped in the fields and some types of homecraft. We learnt about deadly snakes and poisonous fruits long before formal school. We lost most of that knowledge at school and in some ways people are now getting university degrees for re-learning what they already knew for free long ago.

Going back over and over again to the rural areas always produces nostalgia for days gone by. A relative of mine was up well before dawn. The cattle had to go to the dip. The drinking water had to be fetched from the well before the queues began in mid-morning. The door of one hut had to be repaired, and by the time he woke me up about six o'clock he had almost done a day's work.

'Wake up!' he said, 'a man must not sleep so late!' He had already made the fire and was boiling water for washing and making tea. A small pan near the fire was for making popcorn. Somehow one could not help recalling the management rules in conventional workplaces. This man was the planner, the engineer, the carpenter, and manager and all that goes with organisation.

As the sun came up we heard the cry of a desperate child. His father was behind him, a man of about 30 with a stick in his hand. He was mumbling something to the child, but we could not hear what. The child shot past us in the direction of the school. The father joined us by the fire, looking sober, calm and collected. We exchanged greetings and asked what the matter was with the child.

'Well,' he said, 'this son of mine runs away from school. He's doing exactly what I used to do, and look what troubles I have now. I was telling him that if he wants to drive cars like everybody else he must go to school. But unless I beat him he just will not move.'

That event revealed so much. With the best of intentions, the father was probably responsible for the child's hatred of school and learning. I could feel for the child, especially if he had spent the previous evening listening to stories, playing games and perhaps singing and learning much in the midnight classroom. Waking up in the morning to a violent education could only disturb his person.

Perhaps the most important aspect of growing up in a rural community was a sense of belonging, a homeliness that the bigger places cannot provide. The village instilled some human values that can only be felt in that sense of belonging. Many people are spiritually at home in the rural areas. The towns have an in-built transitory feeling. In many ways the trip to the rural areas to perform traditional rituals remains an in-built requirement for town dwellers.

Perhaps traditional story-tellers, who have been imbued with basic knowledge of conservation needs, could do much to spread the message through the midnight classrooms. The songs and games, which create the gay atmosphere, could also be used. Remembering the effect those romantic nights had on me as a child, I feel sure that here is a place in the lives of the people still in touch with the natural world where the conservation ethic can be effectively promoted.

NOTE

1. The assistance of Peter Jackson is gratefully acknowledged.

Chapter Nine

ENVIRONMENTAL EDUCATION IN THIRD WORLD
SCHOOLS - RHETORIC OR REALISM?*

G. Vulliamy

INTRODUCTION

Following the publication of the World Conservation
Strategy, whose main purpose is to 'persuade the nations of
the world to adopt ecologically sound development
practices' (IUCN and the United Nations Environment
Programme, 1984, p.8), many people have understandably
looked to the educational system as the principal channel
for influencing the behaviour of future generations. This
applies especially to schools in the Third World, where
environmental problems of over-population, lack of water,
fuel and food, soil erosion and deforestation are at their
most acute.

The importance of teaching about environmental concerns in the Third World cannot be denied. However, in their
enthusiasm for such endeavours, many First World educators, largely through ignorance of the practical realities and
social context of schooling in such countries, are prone to
initiate policies and projects that are, at best, unrealistic
and, at worst, counter-productive. Consequently, there is a
danger that the lofty ideals of such environmental education
will suffer the same fate in the Third World as that of other
educational reforms such as community schooling (see
Watson 1982) or education for self-reliance (see Cooksey,
1986; Saunders and Vulliamy, 1983) and remain mere rhetoric, divorced from the practical realities of everyday
schooling.

We now have a significant body of research concerning
the implementation of educational reforms in developing
countries. Many of these attempted reforms have much in
common with the aims of environmental educators. We can
therefore identify the major constraints programmes for
environmental education are likely to face. While these will
be the main theme of this article, it should not be regarded
as a recipe for pessimism, but rather for a more realistic

143

appraisal of the implementation task. If is only by understanding the source of constraints that we can adopt the
most appropriate strategies for trying to overcome them.
The discussion is restricted to schooling in Third World
countries and is illustrated with references to the author's
research in Papua New Guinean secondary schools and to
ideas and examples discussed in the Environment Workshop
of the 1985 Bangalore Conference on 'Science and
Technology Education and Future Human Needs'. Since it
was this conference which sowed the seeds of this paper, I
will begin with some brief reactions to it.

THE BANGALORE CONFERENCE

A very positive feature of the conference was that it
explicitly sought to avoid the familiar pitfalls of such
international gatherings on education. These are that policy-
makers, officials from international agencies and academics
deliver papers on the aims of education and on what ought
to be happening, with no regard to the practical realities or
perceptions of those working in school classrooms themselves. Where research evidence is drawn upon it is usually
of a type, such as questionnaire surveys or short visits to
schools, which tends to reproduce the rhetoric of policies
rather than investigating the extent to which that rhetoric
has actually been translated into practice. A danger is that
countries import educational policies and projects from
other countries, with high hopes fuelled by widespread
discussion of such policies at international conferences or in
the literature, despite the lack of evidence of the effective
practice of such policies.

With a conference on the aims of Science and
Technology education safely behind them, the organisers of
the Bangalore conference invited papers providing case-
studies of practice. They also involved classroom teachers
and other practitioners in order to provide a degree of
realism to the discussions that is usually absent. In this I
believe the conference was successful. However, in doing so
it fell victim to a further misguided assumption - namely
that successful examples of curriculum practice are freely
generalisable to different contexts. This assumption was
especially apparent in the Environment Workshop, where the
search was on for examples of environmental education in
practice, together with associated teaching and learning
materials, that had demonstrably worked. Some excellent

144

case studies were presented. However, little attention was paid to the wealth of research material on the implement- ation of educational innovations, that suggests that the mode of implementation must differ depending on the context of the innovation. Thus, not only are there dangers in importing the content of school syllabuses uncritically from the First to the Third World - as is now widely recognised following the experiences of some African countries with the New Maths or with Nuffield Science - but there are also dangers in transferring teaching styles or curriculum development approaches (see, for example, Crossley, 1984).

It appeared to be widely assumed at the Environment Workshop that approaches to teaching about environmental concerns that have been found to be successful either in formal schooling in Western countries or in non-formal, community-oriented projects in the Third World could with little modification be transplanted into Third World schools. Here I argue that such an assumption is erroneous, because the perceptions of schooling in the Third World, together with the economic, political and social context in which it is conducted, present constraints that are very different.

In the following sections of this paper, three broad categories of potential implementation constraints are addressed. The paper then concludes with the positive lessons to be learned by those wishing to see a concern for environmental issues pervade the curriculum of schools in the Third World.

THE SOCIO-POLITICAL CONTEXT OF SCHOOLING IN THE THIRD WORLD

In many colonial countries prior to Independence, the educa- tional system was clearly stratified into highly academic schools for expatriates and schools that the colonisers tried to make relevant to agriculture and local community con- cerns for the majority of the indigenous people. On the one hand, therefore, the route to upward social mobility became clearly identified with a style of academic education that was often totally irrelevant to the countries concerned, being based instead on syllabuses and examinations derived from the metropole. On the other hand, attempts to relate schooling to local community concerns became identified with attempts to keep the colonised in an inferior position. This has resulted in deep-seated attitudes concerning the role of schooling that persist today. Schools tend to be valued extrinsically for their ability to promote mobility out of the subsistence sector to formal sector jobs, via the acquisition of examination certificates, rather than intrinsically for any knowledge or understanding gained within them.

Schools everywhere tend to reproduce the structure of the society of which they are a part. However, it has been convincingly argued that the effects of the 'diploma disease' (Dore, 1976) in distorting the style and content of schooling are far greater in developing countries, because the differentials between the lifestyles of the educationally successful and the unsuccessful are so much greater than in industrialised countries. Any attempt at curriculum reform in Third World schools must recognise that parents and students are likely to reject any innovations which do not accord with the prevalent routes to high status examination success. This has proved to be the major constraint on Third World attempts to vocationalise the curriculum (Foster, 1965; Lillis and Hogan, 1983), to link education with production in self-reliance programmes in Tanzania (Saunders, 1982), to promote non-formal education in developing countries (Simkins, 1977) and to relate the school more to the local community (Thompson, 1983).

The fate of community schooling is particularly relevant in this context because many of its aims and methods, such as project work on local environmental issues, are shared with those of environmental educators. Martin's review of the practice of community schooling in South East Asia notes that 'the community school is more talked about than actually practiced' (1984, p.86). One reason for this relates to factors, such as inadequate training for teachers for the wider range of tasks implied by the concept of a community school, to be considered later. However, the most fundamental constraint is a socio-political one arising from the dualism which the concept of a community school necessarily implies, given the function of formal schooling in the promotion of upward mobility. While the rhetoric is one of the school supporting the interests and aspirations of the community, the irony is that parental aspirations are more usually directed at using the school to promote children out of the community (King, 1976). In such circumstances, any attempt to localise the curricula will be resisted, because it denies opportunities in the competition for certification, which is dependent upon national examinations. This, in turn, affects the motivation of teachers, who recognise not only that their progress is usually judged by the inspectorate purely in terms of their classroom and school performance, but also that community members are unlikely to value their wider contributions to community life. Thus, for example, Seymour's (1974) case study of the Iban in Malaysia illustrates how the community only co-operated with teachers when they helped the children to subvert the community orientation of the school and use it instead as an avenue to formal sector jobs. Similarly, Bray (1983) compares the ambitious aims of the proposals in Papua New Guinea in the mid-1970s, to modify the country's primary schools into community schools, with the ensuing practice. While there were changes in nomenclature, staffing and curriculum, he argues that these developments were minor compared to those which had been originally proposed:

> The institutions are not community schools in the sense that adults learn in them as well as children, and they remain primary schools in that their main purpose is generally considered to be the preparation of pupils for secondary schools. A Community Life syllabus was introduced in 1977, and was intended to combine history, geography and social studies with an active programme of cultural studies that brought the village into the school and took the school into the village. But even this part of the syllabus generally remains academic and classroom based, and it has not matched hopes. (p.38)

THE EDUCATIONAL SYSTEM

Attempts to innovate must also take account of key features of the educational system as a whole. If, for example, curricula are centralised and assessed by national examinations, then pilot curriculum projects in isolated schools are likely to be rejected because students become disadvantaged vis-à-vis those in conventional schools. This, for example, was the fate of the attempt at Swaneng Hill school in Botswana to provide a more relevant curriculum by integrating academic with practical work (see van Rensburg, 1974). Learning from such experience, a positive feature of the Secondary Schools Community Extension Project in Papua New Guinea has been a steadfast attempt to avoid such a dualistic fate, by ensuring that students from its pilot schools compete on equal terms with conventional high school students (see Vulliamy, 1985). Similarly, the addition of new school subjects or learning experiences, even if in all schools, is likely to be rejected if they are not given the same examination status as conventional work.

The style of national examinations tends to be a more important determinant of the content and process of teaching than syllabuses. Research indicates that the vast majority of questions asked in school examinations in developing countries test factual recall, rather than comprehension or application skills (Little, 1982; Oxenham, 1984). This encourages the rote teaching of factual information and places a low premium on the relevance of such teaching to the students' own lives.

Classroom teaching in developing countries therefore tends to be characterised by a formalistic, didactic style (Beeby, 1966; 1980). This is reinforced by the fact that most teachers have themselves had very limited education and training. Since teachers are often unsure of the subject matter they teach, they are frightened of deviating from the syllabus or of encouraging the asking of questions by students. Most of the case studies of environmental education discussed at the Bangalore Conference required that teachers operate at what Beeby has called 'the stage of meaning'. They incorporated elements of 'progressive' teaching styles adopted in the West, such as student-centred learning strategies, project work, discussion groups, drama, games, and simulations, and so on. Empirical evidence, however, suggests that teachers in many developing countries are at what Beeby calls 'the stage of formalism' (Musgrave, 1984; Guthrie, 1980). In such circumstances not only are such pedagogical styles unrealistic, but their attempted introduction, in the absence of a massive inservice training programme to support them, is likely to lead to confusion and demoralisation for teachers. This is well illustrated in Field's (1981) comprehensive evaluation of the 'Generalist Teaching' innovation in Papua New Guinea high schools. Introduced in 1975, but terminated officially in 1979 after major implementation problems, generalist teaching was an attempt to move away from subject specialisation towards subject integration and a more practical, community-oriented approach in the first two years (grades 7 and 8).

Attempts to innovate within schools must also take account of powerful interest groups within the educational system. The school inspectorate, for example, is likely to prove a more potent influence on teachers' behaviour than the ideals of curriculum developers.

A combination of all the factors discussed above culminates in an incentive structure for teachers and students that militates against any deviations from inherited conceptions of teaching and learning. In such circumstances the lofty ideals of educational reformers are likely to be broken down by pressures from within the school itself -from students in the classroom and from teachers in the upper level of the school hierarchy outside the classroom.

When teachers have either resisted innovations or adapted them to their own needs, they have often been viewed as conservative opponents of change. This, however, is misleading, as Hurst (1981) has argued in his discussion of some issues relating to the improvement of the quality of education in developing countries. Resistance to innovation can often be interpreted as an entirely rational response to the reality of the classroom situation. Schools in developing countries are often characterised by very poor resources, by chronic teacher shortages and by organisational problems caused by weak leadership. In such circumstances, the kinds of 'progressive' teaching styles referred to above are likely to be inappropriate, even in those rare cases where teachers have shown that they are confident in using them.

SCHOOL-VILLAGE TRANSFER

Research suggests that, even if schools do effectively teach about environmental issues, there are likely to be major constraints on the likelihood of such teaching influencing students' behaviour outside the school. For the reasons highlighted above, students do not tend to perceive 'school' knowledge as having any relevance to their everyday lives. Moreover, where such 'school' knowledge is explicitly related to the local environment, it often conflicts with indigenous knowledge and felt needs. This can be illustrated by current debates concerning the role of agriculture in contemporary Papua New Guinea.

There is increasing concern amongst conservationists, agricultural experts and extension workers, especially expatriates, that recent developments are promoting a potential crisis for traditional subsistence agriculture in Papua New Guinea. They argue that previous emphases in the country on cash cropping have severely reduced the area of land available for subsistence agriculture, by which the majority of the population lives. Moreover, faster rates of population growth, together with traditional agricultural techniques, especially slash and burn gardening, are putting increasing pressure on finite land resources resulting, for example, in villagers having to walk longer and longer distances to their gardens. Finally, the government has emphasised that the country must significantly increase its domestic food production in order to reduce reliance on imported Western foodstuffs.

Such concerns have led to the promotion of 'improved subsistence agriculture' (ISA) in schools, with an emphasis on more intensive subsistence gardening techniques. These involve numerous approaches not previously used by most Papua New Guineans, such as crop rotation, mulching and composting, grafting and pruning, the avoidance of slash and burn, and so on.

Discussions with staff and students in secondary schools in which I was conducting research suggest that there would be a number of problems with the application of ISA in many villages. These spring from the assumption underlying ISA that the task of increasing the output of subsistence agriculture is purely mechanical, soluble without reference to the cultural, and even technical, context of indigenous agriculture. This failure to recognise the practical and cultural realities of village life means that the successful introduction of new techniques can leave villagers worse off than they were before.

In one school, for example, students complained that the failure to use slash and burn had been responsible for the loss of most of the crops to insects. Such a problem is recognised in the ISA literature, together with the fact that failure to burn the land can result in the loss of important nutrients released by the burning process itself. Counteracting these problems requires the use of both fertilisers and insecticides. These require cash and, anyway, they are not readily available in most villages. Moreover, students report that the use of manure, or even compost, was usually culturally taboo. It should not be surprising, therefore, to find an anthropologist reporting from the field that:

Kaduwagans are sophisticated agriculturalists, and usually know more about local growing conditions than do the experts sent in to help them. As one expatriate expert ruefully told me in 1980, "For years we've been telling them not to burn off their gardens annually. But, you know, that's poor advice, and fortunately they never took it. The reason is the high insect population. Last year I finally tried to practise what I preached and insects consumed the entire crop. (Montague, 1981, p.15)

The cultural consequences of changes in technique usually went unrecognised by teachers, most of whom had no direct experience of village agriculture, being either expatriates or national teachers who had been trained in Western-style techniques at agricultural college. These consequences became apparent, however, on talking to those national staff or mission workers who had intimate knowledge of the local area. For example, moves towards developing intensive piggeries, rather than having pigs roam loose around villages, created numerous problems. In remote Highland communities sending students to a school where such a pig project was taught, the custom of everyone leaving the village for days, or even weeks, at a time for traditional ceremonies was only possible if villagers' pigs could forage freely for themselves during these period. In coastal villages near the school itself, villagers complained that the provision of food, and especially water, for pigs during the dry season meant that any form of intensive piggery was unworkable. Or again, recommendations that changes should be made to more insect-resistant types of taro failed to recognise that in some areas different clans are closely associated with particular varieties of taro, which may even be named after them, and which they would not be prepared to replace with a more productive type.

The rationale for ISA is, as we have seen, that shortages of available land for subsistence gardens will lead to loss of domestic food production and consequent malnutrition. In a few parts of Papua New Guinea, such shortages are already acute and recognised as such by villagers, who then have a direct motivation to introduce new crops or new gardening techniques. The ISA programmes have often been devised from the experience of expatriate agriculturalists and nutritionists, who have worked in such areas. Even in these cases, however, preliminary enthusiasm for ISA has sometimes given way to a more realistic appraisal of the difficulties, and at times inappropriateness, of changing villagers' traditional gardening techniques. Thus, for example, in a postcript written more than a year after a chapter advocating the same use of ISA techniques in Oksapmin in the West Sepik Provence, Cape (1981, p.176) comments that the 'improved' methods he had suggested:

> ... will be less successful than hoped. For, as research continues into the present gardening system, it is becoming apparent that there are good reasons why Oksapmins garden as they do. Also there are several factors which will make it difficult to adopt the improved gardening methods that were designed by a total stranger after a stay of only eighteen months in the area.

However, in many parts of Papua New Guinea there is no intense land shortage. In such circumstances villagers have little incentive to change gardening methods and there are cultural pressures to limit production to that which is sufficient for villagers' everyday needs, but which is far below what is technically possible (for a fuller discussion of cultural constraints upon rural development, see Vulliamy and Carrier, 1985).

The negative knock-on effects of suggested changes are not restricted to the sphere of agricultural techniques. For example, following an anthropological study of primary schooling in Wankung, Morobe Province, Smith (1972) questions the relevance of aspects of the teaching of Western concepts of health and hygiene:

> The teaching of 'health rules' to children is unrealistic. It is physically impossible to assure that bodies and utensils are clean when they are always either on the ground or near it. Classroom lessons about 'clean hands', 'clean food', 'dirt' being 'dangerous' and so on, verifiable as they may be in the opinion of Europeans, are so far removed from the realm of possible alternatives available to Wankung children that they are never made operational ... Further, in a situation where village life satisfies the wants of the villagers, there is little pressure to change, particularly when seemingly

minute alterations in living procedures imply radical changes in lifestyle. For example, in order to keep dust and flies away from food, people would need to begin working <u>inside</u> houses. Such a move would involve Wankung people in a major shift in values; the food of 'real men' is prepared and eaten in full public view. Any attempt to 'hide' food 'inside' may be disruptive of the harmony within the patrilineal descent group (pp.146-147).

CONCLUSION

The first lesson to be learned from the above discussion is that it would be foolish to expect schools to make a significant impact towards solving the environmental problems of a society. Policy-makers worldwide have a habit of expecting schools to help solve problems that are at source social, economic and political. This applies especially in the Third World, where changes in curricula have been adopted with the impossible aim of solving the school-leaver unemployment problem or reducing rural-urban migration. Where schools can play a positive role, however, is in helping reinforce desired changes initiated outside the schooling system. If policy-makers in developing countries can through their actions, as well as through their rhetoric, show a greater concern for environmental issues, then it is important that schools make students aware of the rationale behind such actions.

A second lesson is that if the teaching of environmental issues is to be encouraged in Third World schools, such work must be given high status in the eyes of students and teachers. Any educational innovation must be very sensitive to the specific context in which it is attempted. In countries with the more conventional centralised curricula and examinations, for example, this requires changes in national syllabuses and examinations, together with teaching training programmes to support such changes. It is also likely to require infiltrating environmental concerns into the higher status subjects (such as English, Mathematics and Science), rather than creating new subjects which would inevitably be accorded lower status.

In most Third World schools the single most important reform required to promote environmental education would be a change in examination methods designed to promote this. This is recognised in Glasgow's (1985) analysis of the introduction of environmental education in secondary schools in the Caribbean. While a number of examining bodies in that region have, as elsewhere, already incorporated environmental content into science syllabuses, she makes the claim that it is only in the Caribbean Examinations Council that 'the evaluation strategies leave no alternative but to include environmental aspects in a way that is very relevant to the student' (p.10). In this respect school systems which contain a component of school-based continuous assessment for students, in a manner which actually contributes to their final assessment and future life chances, are at a distinct advantage. Such internal assessment of students allows greater scope for evaluating skills that are likely to be more highly valued by environmental educators than the mere regurgitation of factual content. In one of my Papua New Guinea research schools, for example, students were rated according to the cleanliness of the water emerging from small filtration drums they had constructed, using tin cans, coconut coverings, stones, gravel and sand. However the research also revealed that there were major problems in attempting to extend assessment to evaluate student attributes beyond the more traditional ones (Vulliamy, 1985, pp.154-160). Similarly, Wanasinghe (1982) cites the creation of over-complex systems of internal assessment of students as one of the reasons for the demise of the Pre-Vocational Studies programme in Sri Lankan secondary schools.

The above analysis has identified features of schooling in developing countries which seriously constrain the introduction of approaches to teaching about environmental issues, which have their origin in the West. Environmental educators should temper some of their more idealistic ambitions with the harsh realities of the practicalities of schooling in the Third World.

REFERENCES

Beeby, C.E. (1966), The Quality of Education in Developing Countries. Cambridge, Mass, USA, Harvard University Press.

Beeby, C.E. (1980), 'Reply to Gerard Guthrie', International Review of Education, 26:439-449.

Bray, M. (1983), 'Community schools or primary schools? A reform of the 1970s reconsidered', Yagl-Ambu, 10:35-44.

Cape, N. (1981), 'Agriculture', in Weeks, S.G. (ed.), Oksapmin: Development and Change, ERU Occasional Paper No. 7, Educational Research Unit, University of Papua New Guinea, Port Moresby, pp.149-190.

Cooksey, B. (1986), 'Policy and practice in Tanzanian secondary education since 1967', International Journal of Educational Development, 6:183-202.

Crossley, M. (1984), 'Strategies for curriculum change and the question of international transfer', Journal of Curriculum Studies, 16:75-88.

Dore, R. (1976), The Diploma Disease. London, George Allen and Unwin.

Field, S. (1981), Generalist Teaching Policy and Practice, ERU Research Report No. 36. Educational Research Unit, University of Papua New Guinea, Port Moresby.

Foster, P.J. (1965), 'The vocational school fallacy in development planning', in Anderson, C.A. and Bowman, M.J. (eds.), Education and Economist Development. Chicago, Aldine Publishing Company, pp.142-166.

Glasgow, J. (1985), Syllabuses with Environmental Emphasis in the Caribbean, The Committee on the Teaching of Science of the International Council of Scientific Unions, Bangalore Conference.

Guthrie, G. (1980), 'Stages of educational development? Beeby revisited', International Review of Education, 26:411-438.

Hurst, P. (1981), 'Some issues in improving the quality of education in developing countries', Comparative Education, 17:185-193.

King, K. (1976), 'The community school. Rich world, poor world', in King, K. (ed.), Education and Community in Africa. University of Edinburgh, Centre of African Studies, pp.1-32.

Lillis, K.M. and Hogan, D. (1983), 'Dilemmas of diversification: problems associated with vocational education in developing countries', Comparative Education, 19:89-107.

Little, A. (1982), The role of examinations in the promotion of the 'Paper Qualification Syndrome', in JASPA Paper Qualification Syndrome (PQS) and Unemployment of School Leavers. Geneva, International Labour Office, pp.176-195.

Martin, C.J. (1984), ' "Community school" or the community's school: issues in rural reducation with special reference to South East Asia', Compare, 14:85-106.

Montague, S.P. (1981), 'Kaduwagan attitudes towards formal and non-formal education', Papua New Guinea Journal of Education, 18:1-21.

Musgrave, P.W. (1974), 'Primary schools, teacher training and change: Beeby reconsidered - some data for the Pacific', Papua New Guinea Journal of Education, Vol. 10, No. 1.

Oxenham, J. (ed.) (1984), Education Versus Qualifications? London: George Allen and Unwin.

Rensburg, P. van (1974), Report from Swaneng Hill: Education and Employment in an African Company. Uppsala, The Dag Hammarskjöld Foundation.

Saunders, M. (1982), 'Productive activity in the curriculum: changing the literate bias of secondary schools in Tanzania', British Journal of Sociology of Education, 3:39-55.

Saunders, M. and Vulliamy, G. (1983), 'The implementation of curricular reform: Tanzania and Papua New Guinea', Comparative Education Review, 27:351-373.

Seymour, J.M. (1974), 'The rural school as an acculturating institution: the Iban of Malaysia', Human Organisation, 33:277-290.

Simkins, T. (1977), Non-Formal Education and Development: Some Critical Issues, Manchester Monographs No. 8, Department of Adult and Higher Education, University of Manchester.

Smith, R.A. (1972), 'Education for what?' Papua New Guinea Journal of Education, 8:144-149.

Thompson, A.R. (1983), 'Community education in the 1980s: what can we learn from experience?' International Journal of Education Development, 3:3-17.

United Nations Environment Programme (1984), An Introduction to the World Conservation Strategy, International Union for Conservation of Nature and Natural Resources.

Vulliamy, G. (1985), 'The diversification of secondary school curricula: problems and possibilities in Papua New Guinea', in Lillis, K.M. (ed.), School and Community in Less Developed Areas. London, Croom Helm, pp.142-170.

Vulliamy, G. and Carrier, J. (1985), 'Sorcery and SSCEP: the cultural context of an educational innovation', British Journal of Sociology of Education, 6:17-33.

Wanasinghe, J. (1982), 'Innovation in educational assessment with special reference to educational reforms introduced at the junior secondary level in Sri Lanka in 1972', International Journal of Educational Development, 2:141-152.

Watson, K. (1982), Teachers and Community Schools as Instruments of Rural Development: the Rhetoric and the Reality. Victoria, Australia, International Community Education Association.

NOTE

* This chapter first appeared in The Environmentalist, vol. 7, no. I, 11-19 (1987).

Chapter Ten

ESSENTIAL CONCEPTS FOR ENVIRONMENTAL EDUCATION IN MAURITIUS

M. Atchia

The basic purpose of our research was to sort out those concepts in environmental education that might be considered essential to promoting favourable environmental attitude change. The aim was to prepare a local adaptation of selected concepts for a specific African region (Mauritius), so constructing an instructional instrument valid in that region.

The concepts were initially derived from personal experience (notably in Mauritius), from the literature (mainly Euro-American), and from a survey of African students attending a British University. The list of concepts was selective with some emphasis being given to the theoretical school of Novak, Ausubel et al.[1] which challenges the Piagetian assumption that children cannot grasp abstract concepts, pointing out that this is not because of their abstractness but because the relevant frameworks are inappropriate. For example, in reforms at the Mauritius Institute of Education, it was felt that a whole new conceptual reorganisation of all knowledge was needed rather than the simple addition of local factors to outside models.

In the event a list of 84 concepts was prepared and sent to a panel of experts in the UK and Mauritius. The aim was to find those concepts which were essential in developing an attitude of care and concern for man in his environment in environmental programmes for 5-13 year olds. The respondents were asked to put a number from 1 to 4 in evaluating the usefulness of concepts (4 essential, 3 useful/acceptable, 2 inappropriate/unnecessary, 1 unacceptable/harmful/incorrect). The UK experts panel gave high scores (a mean ranging from 3.3 to 3.3860) to 40 concepts but the Mauritian panel only retained 35 of these. This list of 35 is offered as a representation for the Mauritius situation of essential concepts for environmental education.

A. ECOLOGY

1. The size and range of a population is regulated by available physical resources (e.g. space, water, air, food) and by biological factors (e.g. competition).

2. The flow of energy and material through an ecosystem links all communities and organisms in a complex of chains and webs which invariably start with plants.

3. The planet is made up of a number of interacting and interdependent components.

4. One of the planet's components, the biosphere, is made up of units (ecosystems) which are self-sustaining and require solar energy as their only external resource.

5. We live in 'space-ship earth', a closed system character-ised as having limits.

B. HUMAN ECOLOGY

1. Man's activities and technologies influence considerably the natural environment and may affect its capacity to sustain life, including human life.

2. Man is influenced by many of the same hereditary and environmental factors that affect other species.

3. A mode of life heavily dependent upon rapidly diminish-ing non-renewable energy sources (e.g. fossil fuel) is unstable.

C. HUMAN SOCIETY AND CULTURE

1. Culture (i.e. mode of life) is not static; it changes and evolves.

2. The relations between man and his environment are mediated by his culture (his mode of life and habits).

D. HUMAN SOCIETY AND ECONOMICS

1. Ready transportation, interest in nature, money sur-pluses, shorter working hours, combine to create heavy

pressure on recreational facilities.

2. A clear difference exists between the natural needs of man and those wants and desires artificially created by advertising and social pressures.

3. Economic efficiency often fails to result in conservation of resources.

E. MANAGEMENT OF RESOURCES

1. Rational utilisation of a renewable source (e.g. rate of fish catch equal to rate of natural regeneration of fish population) is a sensible way of preserving the resource while obtaining maximum benefits from it.

2. Sound environmental management is beneficial to both man and environment.

3. Resources use needs long-term planning.

4. Elimination of wastage is important to modern societies, to help reduce resources consumption.

5. The rate of depletion of a non-renewable resource can be reduced by re-cycling and by finding alternatives.

6. Knowledge and techniques from many different disciplines are needed for environmental management.

7. Technology should concentrate on non-polluting, non-exhaustible sources of energy (sun, wind, tides, waves).

F. POLLUTION AND POLLUTION CONTROL

1. Certain artificial contaminants (e.g. radio-isotopes, mercury, DDT) are too long-lived or of such a nature that natural processes are unable to eliminate them readily.

2. Some pollutants, because of their toxicity and persistance, affect essential life-support systems on the planet (e.g. oxygen production by oceanic plankton).

3. Radioactive pollutants may produce genetic effects

which endanger life on the planet.

4.   Air and water pollutions of a serious nature are the side-effects of human industrial activities.

5.   The ocean has become the final dumping place for chemicals, oil, sewage, agricultural wastes, because these follow natural pathways from where they are released to reach the ocean.

G.   CONSERVATION

1.   Wildlife populations are important aesthetically, biologically (as gene pool), economically and in themselves.

2.   Nature reserves and other wilderness areas are of value in protecting endangered species because they preserve the habitats.

3.   Destruction of natural habitats by man is the single most important cause of extinction today.

4.   Destruction of any wildlife may lead to a collapse of some food chains.

5.   The survival of man is closely linked to the survival of wildlife, both being dependent on the same life-supporting systems.

H.   TOWN AND COUNTRY PLANNING

1.   The protection of soils and the maintenance of their fertility are essential factors in the survival of civilisations and settlements.

2.   A vegetation cover (grass, forest) is important for the balance of nature and for the conservation of soil, besides being an exploitable natural resource.

3.   Soil erosion is the irreversible loss of an essential resource (and must be prevented).

4.   The biological and psycho-social needs of man, and his human dimensions, are prime factors to be considered in town and country planning.

5. Cultural, historical and architectural heritage is as much in need of protection as is wildlife.

NOTES

1   Ausubel, D.P. 1968, Educational Psychology. Holt, Richart and Winston, N.Y.

Chapter Eleven

DEVELOPING CONSERVATION AWARENESS AMONGST YOUTH: A CASE STUDY ON THE POWER OF CO-OPERATION

Erna Witoelar

INTRODUCTION

Development problems in general, and environmental management in particular, have always been far more comprehensive than the areas that government mechanisms are able to reach. There are many aspects of resource management that can be well implemented through the participation of the community.

Natural resources conservation, sanitation and waste management, appropriate technology development, regreening, sustainable agriculture, etc. are only some of the environmental aspects which cannot be coped with by conventional instruments of government policies only.

Therefore the community have both the right and the obligation to take part in various stages and aspects of development. Community awareness, responsibility and co-operative efforts are absolutely vital to the conservation and improvement of the environment. Therefore, the management of the environment requires an approach based on public awareness and community participation.

In the Indonesian setting, this phenomenon becomes increasingly clear, and the growth of citizen's groups/NGOs concerned and active in the field of environment has shown an encouraging development in the last decade. Hundreds of NGOs have sprung up throughout the country, speaking up and taking action on environmental issues. Catalytic to this rapid growth have been, among others, the more favourable atmosphere of the New Order, the availability of more information, and the increasing concern among society.

It is worth mentioning that environmental NGOs, defined as 'an organisation which develops in a self-reliant manner, based on its own initiative and desire, within the community, and is concerned with and active in the field of the living environment', are legally recognised in the statutes of the Act No. 4 of 1982 concerning BasicProvisions for the

165

Management of the Living Environment. The Act covers the rights, responsibilities and roles of the community vis-à-vis the government in the field of environmental management.

The elucidation of Article 19 of the Act mentions that these self reliant community institutions include among others:

(a) professional groups, who by the nature of their profession are concerned with and interested in handling environmental problems; like the association of biologists, landscape architects, science and technology journalists, etc.

(b) hobby groups, who have personal motivations in preserving the natural environment, such as nature lover clubs, divers, mountaineers, cavers and bird lovers.

(c) interest groups, whose special interests in development issues can contribute to the conservation and improvement of the environment, among others consumer groups, women's organisations, legal aid institutions, religious groups, community self-help promoters, both in rural and urban areas, etc.

These various NGOs play different roles according to their particular objectives, class orientation or target groups, institutional systems, capabilities and resources available. Particularly in environmental endeavours, these roles range from creating community awareness, advocating environmental issues and community aspirations, to motivating and empowering the community in enabling them to try to solve their own environmental problems locally.

Despite the encouraging growth of community participation, evidenced by increased quantity of active NGOs, much still needs to be done to increase the quality of the movement.

ENVIRONMENTAL NGOs NETWORKING

Previously, environmental NGOs were quite unaware of each others' existence. This caused much ineffectiveness, inefficiency, overlapping and overlooking of activities. Realising this ignorance and the complex nature of environmental issues, the need was recognised by 1978 by ten Jakarta-based NGOs to have a loose forum of communication, with full appreciation of each other's identity and independence.

The Group of Ten (Kelompol Sepuluh) was then founded, and played quite a significant role in increasing the impact of the NGOs' work, through joint press statements and conferences, joint parliamentary hearings, and dialogues with decision makers.

Nonetheless, it was soon felt that Kelompok Sepuluh was not effective enough, especially in areas outside Jakarta. There was a growing need to create a more comprehensive nationwide network that would be able to meet the needs of NGOs in other parts of the country. Recognising this, in October 1980 Kelompok Sepuluh organised the first National Meeting of 79 environmental NGOs from all over Indonesia.

The meeting was successful in identifying more clearly the needs and goals of the environmental movement in Indonesia. One of the results was the decision to establish the Indonesian Environmental Forum/Wahana Lingkungan Hidup Indonesia (WALHI) as the national communication forum of NGOs concerned and active in environment and development efforts.

The relationship between WALHI and its ever-growing participating NGOs is not in the form of strict membership or a vertical hierarchy. Instead, co-operation is based on mutual interests, concerns and goals, through joint programmes that can be ad hoc or longterm in nature.

WALHI's objectives are to increase the NGOs' involvement in environmental efforts, both in terms of quantity and quality, and to bridge possible gaps in aspirations and perceptions among NGOs, between NGOs and the government, also between NGOs and society at large.

To reach the objectives, WALHI serves environmental NGOs in three main areas: operation of a clearing house for information and communication, organisation of training and human resources development programmes for NGOs, and provision of technical assistance whenever needed by the NGOs to develop their programmes.

Within almost six years of its existence, WALHI has organised outdoor Nature Conservation Training programmes, Environmental Impact courses, Environmental Writing/Journalism courses; and several seminars and workshops with topics ranging from environmental issues like pesticide misuse, pollution control, forest conservation, biomass gasification, and urban agriculture; to 'tools for action' topics such as action research, fund-raising from the public, management for non-profit organisations etc.

To serve the NGOs as a clearing house, WALHI provides access to its library and collection of hundreds of posters, caricatures, and other A-V materials; publishes a monthly newsletter, several books and leaflets; and co-ordinates dialogue forums, parliamentary hearings and NGOs' representations.

WALHI also plays the advocacy role in enlightening government officials (in all different levels and sectors) on NGOs' role and potentials, as well as motivating the private sector and business community to support financially the NGOs' community works (with no strings attached) as part of their corporate image-building.

In the field of programme development, WALHI assists NGOs in identifying resources, seeking recommendations/endorsements for NGOs' programmes, managing block grants for NGOs' small projects, facilitating environmentally sound income generating activities, and transfer of breeding technology.

WALHI also stimulates and facilitates NGOs to jointly increase their impact through smaller networks with mutual concerns (pesticides misuse, pollution control, forest destruction, marine conservation).

In pursuing all above mentioned activities, WALHI always co-operates with one or more NGOs, never on its own. Also all participating NGOs are sharing parts of the resources needed.

On the occasion of the 'Spreading the Message' workshop of the IUCN Conference, WALHI shared its experience in developing conservation awareness amongst youth through its outdoor Nature Conservation Training (NCT) programmes. With the strength of co-operation and networking, this programme managed to achieve quite a lot with a relatively small financial resource.

SPREADING THE CONSERVATION AWARENESS

Since 1981, WALHI has organised jointly with local NGOs sixteen week-long outdoor NCT programmes throughout Indonesia, reaching over 600 young members of about 300 hobby group NGOs, mostly youth nature lovers' clubs (see Appendix 1).

These youth organisations are mostly university-based, besides quite a few neighbourhood-based clubs. We see them as potential future decision-makers, and their basic love for nature makes strong motivation to do more for the environment, given enough insight and access to information.

The objectives of this programme were gradually changing from NCT to another, depending on the needs and interests assessed, also on the theme chosen by the local organisers.

In the beginning the main objectives were: first, to develop the love for nature amongst youth; second, to train their ability in living and working in nature, to enable them to organise nature expeditions; third, to train their ability in adjusting themselves to local communities; and fourth, to develop their ability in utilising their expedition or study results for creating community awareness.

Since more and more participants came from youth nature lovers already familiar with nature expeditions, the objectives of the programme were modified. The objective was then to create among the young NGO activitists an awareness and appreciation of the natural environment, while motivating them to become more involved in local conservation efforts. The programme also attempted to provide concrete skills in examining and analysing environmental issues, as well as solving local problems by focussing on specific topics (forest conservation, land rehabilitation, marine conservation, for example).

THE POWER OF CO-OPERATION

NGO Networking

Only the first NCT was organised directly by WALHI, helped by activists of five Jakarta-based NGOs. After that all fifteen NCTs were organised by ex-participants of an NCT. Requests for organising a national NCT programme have to come from NGOs already participating in one of the NCTs and ready to organise it, including mobilising local resources. Usually, the requests came from several NGOs from the same city forming a joint committee.

Everything was decided by the local committee, from the theme to timing, curricula, location, etc. WALHI only facilitated with options of curricula, methods and resources available; helped bridging with these resources, and sent staff to give assistance whenever needed.

Bigger (usually Jakarta-based) NGOs like the Green Indonesia Foundation (YIH), or networks of NGOs with mutual interest like the Volunteers Against Forest

Destruction (SKEPHI), the Indonesian Pesticide Action Network (KRAPP), etc. are sometimes asked to share their experiences with the participants.

Co-operation with Environmental Study Centres (PSLs)

PSLs are university-based study centres with the inter-relationship of development to the environment as their central theme. As with other institutions within universities in Indonesia, PSLs are expected to play a tripartite role, involving teaching, research, and public service. The PSL network concept was developed by the State Minister of Population and the Environmentl (KLH). It is in process of expansion from the original three (dating back to 1971) to 28 now established, to an eventual 42, with at least one for each of Indonesia's twenty-seven provinces.

Each NCT is organised in close co-operation with a PSL (or PSLs) from the region. They helped the organisers in developing the curricula and training method, as well as providing or linking with human resources needed, like experts from other PSLs, government officials, or NGOs' practitioners. In some cases we asked farmers, fishermen, journalists, army instructors, artists, etc. to share with us their longstanding experiences.

Co-operation with Local Government

The relationship that exists between NGOs and the Indonesian government cannot be easily categorised. There are many relationships with various sectors and levels of the bureaucracy, which, though often marked with fluid co-operation, may also be characterised by mutual distrust and suspicion. WALHI, which enjoys the privileged position of being recognised and listened to, more often than not used as a sounding-board, in particular by KLH, sometimes needs to provide (previously non-existent) communication between the NGOs and local governments.

Encouragingly, once the communication has been established, the tensions are eased and co-operation by mutual need is more easily achieved, and maintained, even long after the programme is over.

NCTs are usually supported by local governments in the form of infrastructure, local transportation (sometimes boats or speedboats are needed), radio communications, etc. since almost all NCTs' locations are in the wild, remote areas.

Co-operation with the Private Sector

Since the very beginning, funds for the programmes were raised by and from environmentally concerned corporate/business leaders. It started with the establishment of the Conservation Education Fund, by businessmen previously supporting Operation Drake in Indonesia, which was later further broadened by increasing participation of other business leaders. Eventually it was formalised into a foundation called the Friends of the Environment Fund/Dana Mitra Lingkungan (DML).

DML's fund-raising efforts were conducted in co-operation with WALHI and KLH, also with associations of business leaders, like the Real Estate Association, the Indonesia Chamber of Commerce, the Indonesian Amcham, the Indonesia-Netherlands Association, the Oil Companies Association, etc. It was aimed at small but continuous support from a lot of companies, instead of big sums from a few corporations. The fund-raising drives also endeavoured to create environmental awareness among the private sector, and to implement it within companies.

Funding provided for each NCT varied between 50 to 70% of the total cost, depending on local resources mobilised by the organising NGOs.

The Training Process

The programmes were normally conducted in an informal and participatory method. Participants were usually sleeping in tents, to be close to nature. Seminar-type discussions were held both indoors and outdoors, where participants discussed conservation principles or shared experiences and concerns.

They held outdoor exercises and practices, also conducted field studies, in accordance with the theme of the programme. These ranged from practising the right way to plant trees for soil conservation, diving to plant and monitor artificial corals for the habitat of fish, planting mangroves, making energy-saving stoves and simple water-purification systems, etc; to exercises in photography, search and rescue, planning an expedition, survival in the forest, first aid, making communicative reports, etc. In some NCTs, even developing public speaking ability was requested as a tool for creating awareness.

Efforts were always made to enable them to integrate or interact with surrounding communities. Villagers around a protected area were usually approached to learn about the need to protect the area. In Central Java, the participants worked together with the villagers in making terraces and planting trees for soil conservation.

In North Sumatra NCT participants were taken by local fishermen to visit coastal areas previously available for fishing, now closed and monopolised by a prawn industry. Unfortunately, they couldn't help the local community that time.

Discussion topics varied from one NCT to another, depending on the theme and available resources. The idea that participants (who came from all parts of Indonesia) were learning local problems and solutions from local resources did not always match with availability of expertise. In these cases we had to look for outside resources who had been making studies or working on solutions to that particular problem. When it was not available, we dropped the topic.

A few basic topics appeared in every NCT, like Why Conservation, Harmony Between Conservation and Development (in the beginning called Conflict Between Conservation and Development, but changed after the Evaluation workshop after the fourth NCT), and The Role of NGOs in Conservation. Later the topic concerning legislation on Basic Provisions for the Management of the Living Environment was also always in demand. Other topics varied a lot, even in the first four NCTs where no specific theme was decided upon.

An interesting and encouraging thing (for us) was that the State Minister for Population and the Environment always tried to make time to attend these programmes (he only missed one), however remote the locations were. He came to listen to the participants' aspirations and answer all questions, and it has become a very important asset to the NCTs, because he was always talking to two ears: the NGOs' and the local governments'.

After each NCT, participants usually organised their own expeditions in small groups to nearby areas, developing further their insights gained from the NCT. This made up a total of 3-4 weeks away from home for each of them. These expeditions, as well as the participants' travel to and from the NCT location, were at the participants' own expense. They also brought their own sleeping bags and food. Limited travel grants or subsidies were provided for participants from far away provinces or potential groups with very meagre resources.

The flexibility of the NCTs is not only beneficial. It also has some shortcomings, mainly because sometimes the same mistakes were made by the ever-changing organisers. Choices of resource persons were not always correct. The local organisers were not always disciplined enough to limit or impose the requirements of participants, making some NCTs exceed the 40 participants limit required for an effective programme. The teamwork of different NGOs working together was sometimes not harmonious enough to be maintained afterwards, although efforts were always made to evaluate the programme, including clearing all tensions felt during the programme.

Nevertheless, all these problems were philosophically seen as part of the on-going learning process by the ex-participants, especially the opportunity to make mistakes as organisers in spreading the awareness to their other colleagues.

Follow-up Activities

For WALHI, the biggest problem of this whole exercise is to keep track of participants' follow-up activities which we consider more important than the training itself. Although a lot of effort was made, like maintaining contacts through sending letters and newsletters, and keeping a database of their activities which we always try (frustratingly) to update, we are not even sure of the amount of NGOs still 'alive', never mind what they're up to these days.

However, good news still keeps popping up. From reports we received at WALHI, lots of smaller local training programmes were organised on their own, usually with the continuance of support from local governments and PSLs. Quite a lot of these groups were motivated and moved by their ex-participating members to develop their activities. From merely hiking, mountaineering, diving, speleology, etc. as their hobby, they are taking up more serious and continuous environmental action programmes, joining other existing environmental groups within the network.

With these growing and developing NGOs, WALHI then maintains relations by facilitating different/advanced services. Several 'new' interest groups grew from these previously hobby groups, working from creating community awareness, advocating environmental issues and community aspirations, to empowering the community to try to solve their local environmental problems.

In creating community awareness, NGOs' activities

include information dissemination and awareness building through contests, exhibitions, media exposure, publications, theatre and other cultural media, nature walks and expeditions, talks/seminars/workshops, youth camps and others.

Advocacy work includes parliamentary hearing, dialogues with decision-makers, media campaigns, facilitating investigative journalism, surveys and fact findings, information exposures through meeting or seminars, representation on government working committees/ technical teams, etc.

Motivation of the community is mostly done through community development activities, such as the construction of demonstration plots, dissemination and informal education programmes, legal assistance, monitoring of environmental impact together with the affected community, and others.

Despite the encouraging growth of community participation in environmental management and education, evidenced by increased quantity of active NGOs, much still needs to be done to increase impact of the movement.

Another encouraging development is the snowball effect of private sector environmental awareness. By participating in DML's programmes, they have become more aware of the environmental impact of their own companies' activities. More and more improvements from within were felt, and the latest development was the establishment of an environmental department within the Indonesian Chamber of Commerce, from the national board down to the province and district level. Also more and more industry people, previously staying away as far as possible from the environmentalists, are now willing to have a dialogue with NGOs.

APPENDIX

Nature Conservation Training Programmes Organised To Date

NCT	Time Organised	Location	Participants	NGOs	Theme
I	December '80	Cibodas, West Java	28	28	General
II	March '81	Cibodas, West Java	41	36	General
III	begin Aug. '81	Cibodas, West Java	36	34	General
IV	end Aug. '81	Kaliurang , Yogya	40	40	General
V	Dec. '81-Jan. '82	Padang, West Sumatra	35	22	Agriculture
VI	June '82	Semarang, Central Java	38	31	Regreening
VII	August '82	Lampung, S. Sumatra	35	23	Human Settlement
VIII	Dec. '82-Jan. '83	Wonogiri, Central Java	37	37	Soil Conservation
IX	Apr.-May '83	Bandung, West Java	45	42	Energy Conservation
X	August '83	Samarinda, E. Kalimant	49	29	Tropical Forest Conservation
XI	Dec. '83	Medan, North Sumatra	34	15	Mangrove Conservation
XII	July '84	Manado, North Celebes	28	14	Marine & Coastal Conservation
XIII	August '84	Malang, East Java	40	31	Mountain & Forest Conservation
XIV	Jan. '85	Palembang, S. Sumatra	43	18	River basin Conservation
XV	August '85	B.masin, S. Kalimantan	43	20	Forest & Water Conservation
XVI	Jan.-Feb. '86	Lombok, W. Nusa Tenggr	61	26	Critical Land Rehabitation

633   295

(some NGOs more than once)

Chapter Twelve

DAMS, ENVIRONMENT AND PEOPLE: INFLUENCING THE DECISION-MAKERS IN INDIA

Dilnavaz Variava

HISTORICAL PERSPECTIVE

By the end of 1986, India had constructed over 1500 large dams, making it one of the leading dam building nations of the 20th century. The recurring traumas of famines and floods, the need for irrigation to bring about self-sufficiency in food, and the need for electricity to support India's industrial infrastructure, have provided a tremendous impetus for the construction of dams. When the Bhakra Nangal dam - one of the largest at that time - was completed, Pandit Jawaharlal Nehru, India's first Prime Minister, proudly referred to these projects as 'the temples of modern India'. And in the years after independence these massive hydro-electric and irrigation projects acquired an almost unquestionable sanctity.

COSTS AND BENEFITS: HOW MUCH AND FOR WHOM?

Over the years, the size of the dams has become bigger and bigger - and the financial, environmental and social costs have become correspondingly greater and greater. To obtain approval for such projects, the Planning Commission of the Government of India insists on a minimum cost benefit ratio of 1:1.5. In calculating the costs, social and environmental costs are grossly undervalued, or not taken into account at all. For instance, forests are valued only as a standing crop - and grossly undervalued at that. No value is placed on the recurring loss in terms of fuelwood and fodder, or on the ecological role of the forests or of the wildlife they contain.

Ironically, the millions of human beings displaced by these projects, the supposed beneficiaries of 'development', have been given equally scant regard. Nominal monetary compensation is calculated for the fields and homes they have occupied for generations. When the projects include resettlement, oustees are often resettled in distant areas (as an extreme example, when the Pong Dam was constructed, villagers from Himachal Pradesh, a Himalayan State, were settled in the deserts of Rajasthan),or on inhospitable lands (the oustees of the Pavna Valley still struggle for survival on the barren hill slopes around the reservoir, causing rapid siltation as they plant poor crops on steep slopes). Most tragic of all is the state of displaced tribals. In the remote forest areas in which many of these dams are constructed, tribals have lived for centuries in harmonious balance with the environment - procuring their daily needs from the forests, acquiring no property except perhaps the right to cultivate certain pieces of land, selling no skills or products in the money market, cut off from the totally alien civilisation of India's cities. Overnight they are uprooted. The meagre monetary compensation sustains them for a short while and then they can be seen, disoriented and starving, on the streets of cities which they had never even visualised, let alone visited. Millions of villagers and tribals have already been affected in this way - many more millions will be affected as India taps its water resources. Still others suffer the effects of dam related diseases such as *genu velgum* (knock knees), skeletal fluororis, Japanese encephalitis, etc. Economists and sociologists ask why rural populations must bear the heavy economic and social costs of projects which bring them only sufferings, while the benefits go to the cities?

In purely economic terms too, the costs and benefits of these big dams have left much to be desired. Due to delays in construction schedules and other factors, costs are, on the average, twice as high as originally estimated. Benefits, on the other hand, are far less than originally projected. It has been found, for instance, that the long delays in commissioning hydro projects, and high transmission losses, have made costs per kW higher for hydro power than for thermal or nuclear power. In terms of irrigation potential, less than 75% has been utilised in the case of major dams, as against 92% for minor dams and ground water. The 6th Plan Document itself admits that yields from major investments in irrigation have been disappointingly low at 1.7 tonnes of food grain per hectare instead of 4 or 5 tonnes per hectare as anticipated.

RE-EDUCATING THE WELL EDUCATED

In spite of these problems the construction of these 'temples of modern India' has been continuing unabated because of the psychological conditioning of the well educated -legislators, planners, engineers - that 'big is beautiful where development is concerned, and very big is even better'. It is re-education which constitutes the real challenge to the abilities of those who perceive the socio-economic and environmental disadvantages of these mammoth projects. Vijay Paranjpye in his paper 'Dams: Are we Damned?' has effectively summed up the implicit assumptions of those who proceed with massive projects which affect the destiny of millions of people and thousands of hectares of land, without adequate scrutiny of the socio-economic and environmental costs. They firmly believe that:

(i)   the benefits (direct and indirect) are so large that the increases in costs or delays in completion are easily compensated by the benefits accruing from them;

(ii) that the indirect and direct benefits in case of dams accrue mainly to the poor people in rural areas;

(iii) that the social and environmental costs (undesirable side-effects) are not of a negative character, and that even if they do exist, they are negligible;

(iv) that in the sphere of power generation, hydro power from any dam is cheaper than any other form of commercial energy;

(v)   that technically the cheapest way of impounding river-waters is by building the largest possible dam by reaping the advantages of 'large-scale'.

The erosion of these assumptions and their replacement with alternative modes of development - or even with the possibility that alternatives exist - becomes the first challenge to the educational skills of those who can see the other side of the picture.

In the past two decades some change has been brought about in the unquestioning devotion to large dams as the only answer to the management of India's vast water resources. In the State of Maharashtra, which had the distinction of having 631 out of the 1554 dams constructed up until 1979, people have repeatedly launched agitations against the destruction of their homes, their livelihood and their lifestyle by these projects. In 1976, the Government of Maharashtra finally accepted the demand: 'land for land', and is presently the only State to have created legislation for this. Although much remains to be desired in its implementation, the Maharashtra decision opens the way for similar demands from displaced villagers and tribals elsewhere. All these moves, however, have largely been aimed at securing better benefits for displaced people, but have not questioned the rationale for the very existence of these massive dams. A significant contribution to questioning this rationale has come in the past decade from Mr. B.B. Vora, who was Secretary for Irrigation in the Agriculture Ministry. His forthright pleas for a shift in emphasis from these major projects to small projects and for the tapping of ground water have made a valuable contribution to changing the perspectives of some of his colleagues, and have provided ammunition to intellectuals in other walks of life.

It was not, however, until the Silent Valley controversy broke out in 1977 that the construction of a big dam became a subject for street corner debate. It was also the first time that environmentalists, economists and power engineers joined hands to successfully challenge the myth that social and environmental costs are a necessary, and insignificant, price for development.

THE SILENT VALLEY: A CASE STUDY

Protected over millennia by its virtual inaccessibility, this 8,950 hectare valley of tropical wet evergreen forests forms part of a magnificent block of almost 40,000 hectares of contiguous forest. The Silent Valley itself is one of the few areas in India to have been almost free of human habitation and intervention (not more than three or four trees per acre were felled for railway sleepers; a coffee plantation in the 19th century was started, and almost immediately abandoned).

Here wildlife, which has been almost eliminated from other parts of the country, still survives - the tiger, the nilgiri langur, the giant squirrel and, most valuable, one of the only two viable populations of the lion-tailed macaque, one of the world's most endangered primates. More exciting is the fact that in the dense vegetation are found wild relatives of pepper, cardamom, tobacco, black gram and other commercial valuable species - a genetic resource essential for the survival and development of their culti- vated counterparts - and many medicinal plants which could provide the basis for modern life-saving drugs.

Unfortunately, as so often happens, environmentalists woke up to the existence of this area, and to the devastating effects of the proposed hydro-electric project, at a stage when the project had already been cleared by the Planning Commission for implementation, and, in fact, preliminary work in this respect had already started in 1973. In 1976-77, a Government-sponsored Task Force for the Protection of the Western Ghats recommended that the project be dropped, but anticipating that the odds against this happening were too great, added a series of safeguards if the project were to be implemented.

The Electricity Board's Campaign

Ironically, it was the over-anxious Kerala State Electricity Board which contributed to saving this valley by rushing to the press with its condemnation of the report, and thus drawing the attention of environmentalists to an area which might otherwise, like so many others, have been quietly destroyed. The subsequent ding-dong battle which lasted over six years saw the deployment of all types of armaments on both sides.

The protagonists for the project triumphantly paraded the following facts:

1. That the hydro project, situated in one of Kerala's poorest regions, was an economic necessity for Kerala - generating 500 million units of energy, irrigating 10,000 hectares of land and providing employment for 3,000 people during its construction phase.

2. That the Silent Valley dam site provided an ideal - almost textbook - location for a hydro project, in a state which would have a power deficit by 1985 without it.

3. That every single political party in Kerala had joined forces to demand from the Prime Minister, Shri Morarji Desai, the implementation of the hydro project. (The only other occasion when such unanimity was achieved

was when the Kerala legislators voted an enhancement of their own emoluments!) In fact, no political party in Kerala which valued its votes dared ask for the abandonment of a project so avidly sought by the people of the economically backward Palghat district of Kerala, where it was to be located. The project was cleared by the Prime Minister, on the State Government undertaking to enact legislation ensuring the 'safeguards' listed in the Task Force Report.

4. That the Kerala High Court had cleared the project for implementation.

With the promotions of 22 engineers at stake, as well as many lucrative contracts for timber felling and construction, the Kerala State Electricity Board (KSEB), and its Unions, mounted an 'environmental education' campaign of its own.

Unknown college professors were projected overnight as 'eminent scientists' and directly or indirectly funded to produce no less than six books denigrating the importance of the Silent Valley, and scores of such articles for the local press. The objective was to project to the public, and to key decision-makers, that 'scientific opinion was divided' on the value of this forest.

Words like 'unique' and 'virgin' which had been loosely applied by environmentalists to this valley, in early stages of the campaign, were pounced upon and torn to shreds. Busloads of legislators and journalists were taken to the dam site, already denuded of trees, to show them how ecologically poor the Silent Valley was, and that the campaign was motivated by smugglers and anti-social elements who did not welcome the healthy intrusion of the Electricity Board personnel.

Eminent scientists and environmentalists who called for the dropping of the project were dubbed as imperialist stooges, or cranks who were more concerned about the welfare of monkeys than of men. Officials, especially Keralites, who occupied key positions in the Central Government (including the Chairman of the Central Water Commission, an authority concerned with implementation of hydel projects throughout the country) were assiduously lobbied and provided with distorted information about the biological wealth of the area and the ecological impact of the dam. The sentiments of the local population were whipped up, on the grounds of economic deprivation, so that environmentalists who went there ran the risk of physical assault if they advocated dropping of the project.

The Environmentalists' Campaign
Environmentalists, on their part, mounted an unprecedented national campaign to create public pressure for stopping the project. Starting in 1977, when a few naturalists in Kerala visited the area after reading the KSEB-sponsored barrage in the newspapers, the campaign gained national momentum by 1979 with 'Save Silent Valley' groups springing up in different parts of the country. The key elements of this campaign were the following:

1. A group of intellectuals in Kerala, who became concerned with the implications of the Silent Valley hydroelectric project, began expressing this through newspaper articles and speeches. Among these were scientists, poets, economists and political activists. The seeds of public debate on the wisdom of the project were planted.

2. The Executive Committee of the Kerala Shastra Sahitya Parishad (KSSP) was inspired, primarily through the persuasions of one of its members, Professor M.K. Prasad, to undertake a 'techno-economic, socio-political' assessment of the implications of the Silent Valley project. The report produced by its multi-disciplinary Task Force, consisting of a biologist, an electrical engineer, a nuclear engineer, an economist and an agricultural scientist-cum-economist, provided a turning point in the Silent Valley campaign. It exposed the undesirability of the project, not only on ecological grounds, but on technical, economic and social grounds.

   While the little grey booklet would have found few customers from the general public, its cogent analysis provided environmental activists with important data, namely: that the energy contribution of the SV project was really marginal in the context of Kerala's power requirements, that alternative sources for augmenting power existed, that ground water provided an effective and economic source for irrigation, and that far more employment could be generated in this economically backward region through medium and small scale industries than through this one major hydro project. More

183

important, it convinced the 60-member Executive Committee of the KSSP to take up the fight to save the Silent Valley.

The KSSP's 7000 members - consisting of teachers, doctors, engineers, lawyers, scientists, agriculturalists, trade union workers and others, all of whom were committed to taking science to the people as a tool for social uplift - were an invaluable weapon in the battle to save the Silent Valley. These members, and especially some of the leading intellectuals of the KSSP's Executive Committee, encouraged and participated in public debates in different parts of Kerala. The youth, especially the college-going youth, were convinced.

Through its unique annual Jatha - a 37-day marathon march from one end of Kerala to the other - KSSP members focussed on the effects of deforestation through traditional cultural media like dance, drama, poetry, music etc. The Jatha covers 300 to 400 villages along its 6000 km route.

3. Eminent scientists, and nationally or internationally renowned environmentalists, were persuaded to make public statements regarding the importance of preserving an area like the Silent Valley in a country which had already lost most of the genetic wealth that such areas represent. Members of the Government-sponsored Task Force on the Western Ghats were persuaded to state that they had been mistaken in recommending the so-called 'safeguards', which had been misused to negate their substantive recommendation that the project should be dropped and the area preserved. They also stated that the safeguards could not really prevent major ecological devastation of the area, but were only an attempt to save what remained, on the assumption that the project could not be dropped. The national press was constantly fed with such information by the Save Silent Valley Committees in Bombay and Madras.

4. International and national organisations like the IUCN, WWF, Bombay Natural History Society and natural history societies in other parts of the country, Friends of Trees and other organisations adopted resolutions, lobbied through members' letters and made representations to the Central and State Government.

5. A court case, though eventually lost, brought an invaluable stay on KSEB operations, thereby providing time for the education campaign to have full effect.

6. Key decision-makers in the government were convinced of the importance of saving Silent Valley - or, at least, of keeping the options open till a future date, when all other power-generating options in Kerala had been exhausted. They become the most valuable forces in stopping the Silent Valley hydro project.

Dr. M.S. Swaminathan, who was then Secretary for Agriculture, Government of India, prepared a report highlighting the genetic wealth of the area and the desirability of postponing the project until this resource could be studied and tapped. Mr. E.M.S. Namboodripad, Secretary of the powerful (in Kerala) Communist Party of India (Marxist), left the matter open for debate within the Party, having been convinced that the proposed hydro project was not an unmitigated blessing for the people of the area.

Above all, Mrs. Indira Gandhi, who became Prime Minister in 1980, played a critical role in asking the State Government to halt further work until the Central and State Governments could explore the implications of the proposed hydel projects and the alternatives that were available. A Committee with representatives of the Central and State Governments was set up by her, under the Chairmanship of Professor M.G.K. Menon (then Secretary, Department of Science & Technology), to look into the ecological implications of the project.

The Outcome
In November 1983, the Silent Valley hydro-electric project was officially declared to have been shelved. Steps have been initiated to create the Silent Valley National Park.

It is difficult to precisely pinpoint all the factors that contributed to the shelving of the Silent Valley hydro-electric project at the eleventh hour and in the face of formidable odds. Many aspects, especially in the realm of human motivations, will always remain as 'grey areas' and conjectures. But if an objective criterion is required that the environmental education campaign worked, it is to be found in the fact that there was no outcry in Kerala when the project was eventually dropped. In the Palghat district of Kerala where the project was to have been located, and

185

where those who called for the dropping of the project had once to face the possibility of physical assault, the people suggested to the KSSP activists that a felicitation be held for the Prime Minister for dropping the project!

INSIGHTS FROM THE SILENT VALLEY CAMPAIGN

In the context of an environmental campaign which covered all segments of society, from three successive Prime Ministers to the peasants affected by the project, what insights can be shared?

The Message

1. 'The decision-maker' is not a single entity - whether Government officer or even Prime Minister. Often the decision making process is a complex inter-relationship between various power groups - e.g. planners, legislators, technocrats - and the people affected. A major requirement of such a campaign is a constant sensitivity to what is the most appropriate message, to whom it should be addressed, and by whom.

2. The message should appropriately combine intellectural arguments and emotional overtones. The former would generally take precedence for decision-makers in the bureaucracy, the latter for the general public.

   (For instance, in the case of Silent Valley, lion-tailed macaques were useful in obtaining support from international and national conservation bodies, but counter-productive at the local level. The 'genetic treasure house' concept was effective for both decision-makers and the general public.)

3. Above all, the environmental education effort must start with an effort to understand the needs of the local people and project how the proposed conservation movement is directly beneficial to them - and/or how the proposed development project will harm them.

The Medium

1. Since the dropping of a project involves convincing many different levels in the decision-making process,

different media have to be used. It is also essential that the selected medium be one that is well respected by those who are to be influenced.

At the Prime Ministerial level, letters from such an eminent naturalist as Dr. Salim Ali, the report prepared by Dr. M.S. Swaminathan and representations from reputed international conservation bodies carried weight. At the popular level, the use of the press created national interest in the fate of the Silent Valley.

In Kerala itself, it was a combination of press reports and of public debate that had the maximum impact. The KSSP's annual Jatha took the issue of deforestation to the countryside. An unprecedented drought in 1983 made the effects of deforestation a living reality for the people of Kerala. A special 12 day Jatha was organised during April/May 1983 covering all districts in Kerala which still had forests. Signatures were collected from 200,000 people asking the Government of Kerala to have a moratorium on all development projects in forested areas and to stop all clear felling, especially on steep slopes.

2.   The decision NOT to use a particular medium is often as important as a decision to use it.

At the State level, representations from international conservation bodies, with their headquarters in Western countries, would have been counter-productive because of the prevailing Communist ethos in this State, and were not used. Similarly, an excellent little pamphlet produced in English and in the local language, Malayalam, for the legislators of Kerala was never used for this purpose since an over-obliging printer had done the job, free of cost, on such exquisite art paper that it would only have helped confirm the allegations of those who contended that the campaign was a capitalist-funded plot!

A 35mm film on which one of our Committee members had laboured for days and nights was never released for screening to millions of people through the Films Division because, by the time it was ready, the campaign had moved into a phase of behind-the-scenes diplomacy rather than public outcry.

In the final stages of the campaign, key officials in the Central Government were looking into alternatives, and trying to find a possible solution. In a four-hour discussion with the initially hostile Chairman of the Central Water Commission, it was decided that the best strategy would be to have a halt to the public controversy so that positions would not harden further, and the Central and State Governments could work on resolving the problem in the right atmosphere. There was accordingly an immediate de-escalation in the press campaign on the part of environmental groups, and a corresponding de-escalation on the part of the supporters of the Electricity Board.

3. At all times, if the medium is treated only as a tool in achieving the larger aims of the campaign, and if the cause takes precedence over individual ego needs, the choice of the appropriate medium usually becomes self-evident.

Methods and Strategies
The following strategies could prove useful in similar campaigns elsehwere:

1. Having a multi-disciplinary report, so that the benefits of the project itself can be questioned. Economic considerations generally take precedence over ecological ones, always putting the 'burden of proof' on conservationists. If environmentalists can convince a few of their colleagues from other disciplines to help them assess the true costs and benefits from proposed 'development' projects, they can shift the ball to the other court.

2. Leading the supposed beneficiaries of development projects to look at and question the benefits which the project promises to bestow. Without this, it is difficult for economically deprived people to sympathise with environmental positions which require them to sacrifice even small short-term gains in the interest of sustainable development. Ironically, in India, even those who will suffer from a project and reap no benefits are

often willing to accept this suffering as a necessary sacrifice to be made in the interest of national development!

3. Asking for a 'postponement' of the project until other alternatives have been exploited, or until the environmental and other implications have been studied, rather than demanding a dropping of the project. It must be appreciated that not only do various lobbies and pressure groups exist, but even 'government' is not a monolithic structure: the objectives of the State Government may be different from those of the Central Government, a 'Development' department would have different objectives from an 'Environment' department, and each creates pressures for fulfilling its own objectives. It is therefore very difficult for those who have ultimately to take the decision to announce officially the dropping of a project. Often they have to play a delicate balancing act between various power groups. For environmentalists to insist on an official statement that a project has been abandoned may only invite vehement pressure for its implementation, and could therefore be counter-productive.

    Mrs. Gandhi, during each of our visits to her, stressed the need to produce particularly acceptable alternatives. She expressed her dilemma most vividly during our meeting with her just before her re-election when she said that 'Once a project is announced in a certain area, it is very difficult to drop it. Local people will behave the way that children do about a toy. They will not listen to arguments, only say: 'I want it, I want it!'.

4. Time and energy expended in convincing key decision-makers, either directly or by using the good offices of those in whom they have confidence, is invaluable. Government officials who do not have a vested interest in a project, either in terms of potential income or prestige, can be most helpful. Those who have an open mind should not be blamed if the pro-project lobby does a better job of communicating with them than environmentalists do.

5. Good rhetoric is not a substitute for hard work and good data in convincing such decision-makers.

In fact, the Chairman of the Central Water Commission strongly resented the last-minute delay in the implementation of the project on vague environmental grounds, and it was not until he had received satisfactory answers to the many distorted facts fed to him by the KSEB that he suggested de-escalation of the confrontation through the press on both sides.

6. Though the 'ultimate' decision-makers' personal interest is invaluable, it does not provide for a simplistic solution to such a politically-sensitive problem.

7. The press can play a crucial role where literacy is high. In other situations, the people have to be approached through more direct contact. Where a science-for-the-people movement as effective as the KSSP does not exist, environmentalists must take the trouble to convince other organisations working in the field of rural uplift to take up their cause.

8. Constant communication and co-ordination in strategy formulation and de-centralisation in action are most effective for powerful campaigning.

Although Silent Valley groups had sprung up spontaneously and independently in different parts of the country, a division of functions emerged. Groups in Kerala created public awareness in their respective areas, the Friends of Trees unit in Kerala pursued the court case, the Society for Environmental Education in Kerala (SEEK) worked largely with children's groups. The Save Silent Valley Committee in Trivandrum, capital city of Kerala, provided a meeting point for important activists from different walks of life and from different political parties.

The Save Silent Valley Committee in Bombay, the most active group outside Kerala, provided support to the efforts in Kerala. This consisted primarily in providing access to the national press, particularly important when the local press stopped giving exposure to the environmental point of view. It also played an important role in approaching eminent scientists and decision-makers in the Central Government and in keeping communications flowing between different groups for effective strategy formulation and implementation.

9. The ability to respond with speed and flexibility to rapidly changing situations is very important in contending with strong, and financially powerful, vested interests involved in such a major project. Established conservation bodies, with their multi-tiered organisation structures, can often be less effective in responding to the demands of a rapidly evolving situation.

    An ad hoc group, like the Save Silent Valley Committee, Bombay, strongly focussed on a single environmental issue, with no hierarchical structure and no requirement to perpetuate itself once the campaign was over, could draw together interested members from various organisations and pool their valuable contracts and expertise. It included people who were actively involved in larger and more permanent conservation bodies. Loose networking could therefore take place on an informal level.

CONCLUSION

The Second Citizens Report on the State of India's Environment, 1984-85, published by the Centre for Science and Environment, sums up the implications of the Silent Valley Campaign as follows:

> The Silent Valley controversy marks the fiercest environmental debate in the country and is likely to establish a precedent wherever any major development project - particularly a dam -threatens the ecological balance ... What Silent Valley has achieved, therefore, is to lay down a new paradigm: development without destruction.

There has been one other successful campaign after Silent Valley. In the case of the Bedthi Project in Karnataka, a group of concerned citizens - scientists, economists, sociologists and legal experts - prepared a well reasoned memorandum successfully challenging the cost benefit ratio for the project and highlighting the socio-cultural and environmental disturbance which the dam would create. The affected farmers provided assistance in data gathering and were vocal in their protests. The Government of Karnataka, which contained officials who were sympathetic, appointed a special Bedthi Committee and ordered a public hearing on the subject. The project was dropped on the basis of the Committee's recommendation and after the Indian Institute of Public Administration, Hyderabad, endorsed the findings of the voluntary group.

Similar battles have been, or are, taking place in other parts of the country. The cost of each such battle, however, is enormous in terms of utilisation of a very scarce resource - namely available manpower for assessing the implications of each project and co-ordinating the campaign for its abandonment.

It is therefore essential that efforts be made at this stage to create a more favourable climate in which future environmental and social education campaigns can be fought. While the battle against the Goliaths of tomorrow continues, there is therefore a crying need for journalists to highlight the by-products of the projects of yesterday - namely the economic loss, ecological destruction and human misery that is the legacy of some of the projects which may have already been implemented.

Simultaneously there is a need for environmentalists to join hands with other citizens' action groups to demand such fundamental rights as the right to information, and the right for those affected to be participants in the implementation of decisions which fundamentally affect their lives.

Wherever individuals have access to key decision-makers personally and through the press, the technological myth that 'Big is beautiful ... and the more complex, the better!' needs to be questioned and debunked.

By relying on hard work and expertise rather than on rhetoric, environmentalists, economists and others could ask for the right to work with government in assessing which projects are in ecologically or socio-culturally less sensitive areas and which ones have high social and environmental costs demanding their re-assessment or modification.

In these ways the ground may gradually grow more fertile for projects that harmoniously fulfil both the development and environmental imperatives which must increasingly be perceived as a shared human concern.

Chapter Thirteen

ENVIRONMENTAL EDUCATION THROUGH MASS MEDIA IN ECUADOR

Yolanda Kakabadse

BACKGROUND

Ecuador is a small country of 270,000 km², with a rapidly growing population that has now reached 8,000,000 inhabitants, and subject to the same environmental problems that affect several other countries of Latin America: a strong tendency to exploit unmercifully the natural resources for economic purposes, very little awareness about the negative effects of this exploitation, and little attention paid to the need of seeking public participation in the solution of these and other problems.

Needless to say, the social and economic problems are not different from those found in all the other countries of the Northern Andean region. The community had not organised itself to deal with these problems and to confront the official organisations to initiate effective actions towards the protection of the environment. A small group of citizens that later on organised themselves to start an official group were the first to assume responsibilities in this area and start a citizen group.

Fundacion Natura is a private Ecuadorian non-profit organisation dedicated to the protection of the environment and to promote among government officials and economic leaders a rational exploitation of natural resources keeping balance with the economic needs of the country. The organisation was created in 1978, through the effort of a small group of Ecuadorians that represented different professions, organisations, and economic activities. It was the first group of its kind created in the country.

Without the need of undertaking a study, it was evident to Fundacion Natura and to the rest of the country that there was little awareness on the subject of the environment, and that national plans had not given much attention to the need to rationalise the use of the country's natural resources.

This group, though, was to face the most serious problem of all. There was little information available and little interest on the part of the decision-makers in the subject. This fact led Fundacion Natura to start its activities with a project addressed to the decision-makers, its main objective being to raise their awareness of the state of the environment in Ecuador.

The name of the project was EDUNAT I and it was the first experience of Fundacion Natura and of Ecuador in environmental public awareness and education.

Mass-media experts, journalists and active professionals in the field of mass communication faced the same problem Fundacion Natura did. They were all interested in an active participation but lacked adequate information and knowledge of the subject to allow them to interpret through mass media the different deeds that were taking place in the country.

Fundacion Natura was lucky enough to find a positive response from the first potential donor approached: USAID. The project was to be implemented in three years and had a total cost of $360,000.

THE PROJECT

The project was designed by a group of Ecuadorian professionals who had a clear idea of the country's needs, and by a mass-media communication expert, Dr. Marco Encalada. It is also important to consider that even though there was no experience in environmental education, the team had a vast knowledge of the patterns of behaviour of the different ethnic groups that form Ecuador. It must also be stated that even though Fundacion Natura had learned about the existence of several environmental education projects in other regions of the world, and believed that some of the ideas could be useful, it definitely rejected the imitation or adaptation of such models.

This strategy brought with it an important positive result: the project itself would train the different members of the team, and the evaluation processes would determine the successes and mistakes of the project design. It was obvious that maybe some of the money could have been better used in the project, but considering all the process, the mistakes could be considered as a positive step for future designs and implementations.

The project was designed to bring the participation of

all mass-media communications into it: newspapers, radio, television, cinema, and little media (leaflets, posters, pamphlets, etc.). It emphasised the importance of reaching decision-makers with the correct message. Politicians, government officers, congressmen, the army, industrialists, and other leading groups were considered to be decision-makers. They were to become target groups of the project.

The general public was important also as it was necessary to simultaneously promote public pressure on certain issues, while different approaches were being made towards community leaders.

Ecuadorian constitutional and governmental structure provide some legal instruments and mechanisms to protect the environment and to punish any attempts against it. Nevertheless, until 1979, when the EDUNAT project started, no priority had been given to these aspects and no provisions, such as regulations, had been considered to implement these laws.

Fundacion Natura in no way wanted to substitute or take the responsibility for these provisons, but to put some pressure on the existing bureaucratic organisations to have them implement or fulfil their obligations. Fundacion Natura had made it very clear, since its creation, that in no way would it take in its hands the obligations or responsibilities assigned to those institutions. On the contrary, maintaining a very low profile, it managed to co-ordinate actions of other institutions and to have their directors consider these subjects as programmes that must be dealt with in the coming months or years.

THE STRATEGY

The first stage of the project was dedicated to the collection of information related to the state of the environment in the country. The idea was to get the most fundamental and vital information which would catch the attention of the people because of its relationship with the most important day to day issues. A team directed by an ecologist travelled all over the country pointing out the most outstanding facts in each area, province and town. This information was to be not only important for an ecological study that was being prepared, but to illustrate several testimonial audio-visuals that were going to be presented to the general public.

All information obtained was compiled in a document

called Main Environmental Problems of Ecuador, published in 1980 and widely distributed within Ecuador. Simultaneously, Fundacion Natura started another project a few months later, 'The Environmental Profile of Ecuador'. To be able to fulfil it, it was necessary to gather and analyse all the existing information on natural resources: watersheds, energy, forestry, pollution, national parks, fauna and flora, institutional responsibilities, etc. The parallel development of both projects favoured the possibility of disseminating, through mass-media, a much wider spectrum of information to the general public.

Before this process started, the general knowledge of the public was measured through several surveys. Enquiries were made in relation to what the Ecuadorians knew about their environment, the problems that were affecting them, what solutions were envisaged and which institutions were responsible for their solutions.

Another important aspect of Fundacion Natura's strategy was that in no way should it approach the general public with only the negative aspects of the present environment, but that it should also point out the wonders of the still preserved areas in all regions and the few actions that had been taken in the past to protect, or prevent or repair the damage to, the environment. In this way, the image of Fundacion Natura was not of an institution that loaded the citizens with problems that apparently had few or no solutions. On the contrary, it was necessary, as part of the strategy, to convey a message of faith and trust of public participation acting for the survival of future generations.

NEWSPAPERS

As mentioned before, journalists of all mass-media representatives were subject to the same problem that affected all other citizens of the country: there was little information available and most important of all, few people could interpret the technical information at hand. To solve this problem, a seminar was designed to which a group of 40 mass-media people were invited. The number of participants was limited by available funding. All of them were chosen from the most important television and radio stations, and the main newspapers and magazines with widest distribution.

The seminar was designed to provide assistants with sufficient knowledge about the main environmental issues of the country, and with basic technical information that would permit them to interpret and process environmental reports.

A special file was prepared for each one of them and an evaluation was made at the end of the seminar to measure the importance that it had for each one of the participants, and to learn about their suggestions and recommendations for future events of the same kind.

The most important objective of this seminar was to interest mass-media people in the environmental subject so as to have them contribute in mass-media communications with whatever information Fundacion Natura and other similar institutions would produce in the future. The results were very interesting: the participants at the seminar started creating the 'Association of Environmental Journalists'. Not only has it become a very important element in the process, but it has on its own initiative, reproduced the seminar in other towns of the country. Another interesting result has been that the most important newspapers of the country have dedicated a permanent space to deal with matters relating to environmental and natural resources management. Quite often the article is produced by a journalist of the same press agency. On other occasions it is a reproduction of a press release produced by Fundacion Natura.

From the beginning of the project (1980), Fundacion Natura hired a full time journalist in charge of producing press releases once or twice a week. As mentioned before, the articles not only emphasised negative but positive aspects of the Ecuadorian environment. Another responsibility that the journalist had was to measure the amount of articles on aspects related to the environment that had appeared in the main newspapers of the country in the year before EDUNAT I started, and to keep track of the ones that would be published in the future. The difference from one year to the other was 50 to one.

After a survey, it was also considered important to reach the general public of the large and most important private and public institutions of the country. Research was carried on to find out about the system of internal communications that each institution had. After that, an agreement with each one of them allowed Fundacion Natura to produce news releases focussing on the main objectives of these institutions, and adapting the style of each news release to one of the internal bulletins or newsletters. Needless to say that each one of the public relations officers of each institution was thankful to receive this contribution.

An additional activity, as far as written material is concerned, was the production of posters that contained information on a topic, an issue or a problem, illustrated with several photographs, and which were distributed and placed in key places in the towns and institutions: supermarkets, cinemas, bus stations, department stores, hospitals, health centres, banks and the regional offices of the Ministries of Education, Health and Agriculture, etc.

RADIO

As happens very often, radio stations in our country are short of cultural/educational programmes of public interest. After a survey, Fundacion Natura decided to produce a series of radio programmes with easy to understand interpretations of every day actions that were affecting the environment.

In a country where there is 12% illiteracy, radio is the most important medium, especially in rural areas.

Fundacion Natura signed a contract with CIESPAL (Centro Internacional de Estudios Superiores de Comunicacion para America Latina), an institution that has a first quality radio laboratory, trained personnel and a school for radio speakers and programmers. A short workshop was held for the radio programmes on environmental issues. An agreement was signed by both institutions for the production of a series of 18 five-minute programmes on different environmental concepts. The style of ten of these programmes was to be that of a light dialogue through which an issue was described briefly discussing its issues and effects.

The next eight programmes were presented in the style of soap opera: the mismanagement of natural elements brought along a tragic incident within a family nucleus, or in other cases an experience that took place in a natural surrounding was the cause of a happy end love story. The reaction of the public towards this last format was evidently a great success, which can easily be understood by the idiosyncrasy of our people.

At the moment, and as part of the second environmental education programme that Fundacion Natura has undertaken (EDUNAT II), 60 additional programmes have been produced. They have a new format in which one character, who is always the same, undergoes several experiences where there is always something new to learn about the environmental and natural resources.

This time, as in EDUNAT I, 100 radio stations of different regions in the country have contributed at no cost to the transmissions of the programmes on a daily basis. In some cases transmissions are twice a day.

The selection of the 100 radio stations was made after a study that provided information about the percentage of listeners and the geographical range that each one covered.

The content of each programme is programmed for an audience that has little or no information about technical terminology.

As the programmes were produced by the radio school (CIESPAL teachers and students) public credit was given to all. Fundacion Natura's responsibility was to provide technical information on different environmental issues and problems of Ecuador. The students, guided by technical staff, were in charge of the elaboration of the scripts of the programmes, which were later approved by Fundacion Natura's staff. The degree of interest created within the radio school has led them to continue producing additional programmes on these subjects, even though the agreement with Fundacion Natura is over and there are not additional funds to support their personal effort.

As mentioned before, radio stations were requested to contribute at no cost to the dissemination of the programmes. All not only accepted gladly but signed a 'contract' with Fundacion Natura through which they committed themselves to pass the programmes in an established timetable for a period of twelve months. The hundred selected radio stations fulfilled their obligations. Copies of the programmes were distributed at no cost to them with a small publicity that gave a brief summary of the content of each programme. Reproduction of the cassettes was also made by CIESPAL, lowering the costs to a minimum.

AUDIO-VISUAL

1. A very sophisticated programme of audio-visuals was elaborated to approach individually the leaders of the country. From a development perspective, five areas were addressed: health, education, industry, labour and exloitation of natural resources. Three screens, six slide projects, first quality slides and well selected music

produced a very attractive show that dealt with each of these areas. Only one was presented at a time, depending on the object of the presentation. Members of the board of Fundacion Natura would be ready to answer questions or make remarks before, during or after the show.

Evaluation showed that the different authorities to whom the show was presented felt that it was up to them to change things through an active participation; that the solution of the problem dealt with in the show was in their hands, also that if the problem had not been dealt with before, it was time to start through their direct participation in policy making or implementation. It was also considered that the problem was affecting important groups of inhabitants and therefore the solution would bring about important social benefits.

With each presentation, the authorities would receive some printed summarised information that contained basic data that would support any follow-up action.

Later on, the same audio-visuals were presented to small groups that could start dialogues and discussions on the subject. Special attention was given to university students, and professional associations, such as lawyers, economists, medical doctors, teacher associations, engineers, etc. Equal attention was given to clubs like Jaycees, Rotary, etc. When we want to describe the impact of these audio-visuals on the public, we say 'Well, they talk about it at cocktail parties!'

2. Other audio-visuals in a much simpler format were produced to reach the general public, through schools, universities, factory personnel, clubs and whichever group requested it.

    Fundacion Natura trained a small group of volunteers, but whenever it was possible it was requested that one of the members of the group to whom the audio-visual was to be presented would make the presentation. Each audio-visual has a printed text which made its presentation easy.

    The subjects dealt with in these audio-visuals were: main environmental problems of the country, water pollution, national parks, forest fires etc. There were also some audio-visuals that had been produced abroad

(WWF for example), that dealt with resources or problems found also in Ecuador and that obviously fulfilled the same purposes.

At the moment, there is an average of ten requests in a week in Quito, and also in Guayaquil (the largest town in the coastal area, where Fundacion Natura has an office).

Since 1980, Fundacion Natura has made a great effort to obtain and exchange audio-visual material with the other Andean countries of the northern region, considering that the many environmental problems are not only alike but have the same origin due to the similar economic, social and political situations that had characterised them during the last centuries. From the NGO point of view, the patterns to solve these problems must also, in some way, be shared to motivate similar local projects.

The different audio-visuals served another important purpose: they were used as base material to initiate round tables, conferences and panels. The levels of each one of them differed according to the audiences. But as a whole, the purpose was to discuss solutions where the general public would be involved. It was important to see that the reaction of the general public was not to elude responsibility and put it in the hands of the governmental organisations, but to organise themselves and fill in the gaps that were obvious in public administration.

MOVIES

Five movies (of six minutes each) were produced to reach the general public of urban areas. Each one of them dealt with a specific problem of the country (erosion, water contamination, fauna and flora, urban ecology and development).

The scripts of the films were also peculiar to the project and to the country's experience. The contents tended to be more emotional than technical. The technical staff of the project considered that it was more important for that moment to motivate people and to touch their feelings rather than their intellectural reaction to the different problems.

Each one of the films emphasised the present young generation and their future and in many ways placed in the present adult generation the responsibility of the definitions of policies, development projects and other activities that concern the future of the natural resources and the environment. Much attention was also given to national parks and reserves, as well as to endemic fauna and flora species. For the first time, this subject was being mentioned through mass-media (except for Galapagos) and a large percentage of the population found out for the first time that there were other areas, many of them in a nearby site, that could offer recreational, scientific and educational activities and information.

Great care was taken in the production of scripts to present the problems together with some alternatives or solutions. It was important in the strategy to convey the message that the problem was not always irreversible.

Once the films were produced, Fundacion Natura managed to have theatre and cinema owners in Quito and Guayaquil agree to transmit one film together with the previews and before the main film. This process lasted a whole year.

The films were copied also in 16mm and in video, therefore they could be used as material for conferences or television shows, or for educational purposes in schools.

An interesting process started after this experience. Film and television producers took an interest in the subject and several additional documentaries were produced. Financial support came not only from private enterprise but from governmental departments.

TELEVISION

National television was fulfilling two purposes. The first was the transmission of a weekly programme referring to fauna and flora, nature and other related subjects.

This programme was rented and transmitted by Fundacion Natura with the financial support of several private enterprises. Even though the names of the supporters appeared at the beginning and end of every programme, there were no commercial interruptions.

Soon this presentation became the number one programme of Saturday night. The income from this programme covered, and still does, the cost of transmission and the monthly administrative costs of Fundacion Natura.

There was evidently a large interest among the population in learning more about environmental subjects not only in Ecuador but worldwide. About 50% of the new members informed that they had learned about Fundacion Natura through the television programmes. Unfortunately, available films in the market referred mainly to Europe, North America and Africa. Little has been produced about South America, and out of that only a few have been translated into Spanish.

In the last three years, the five television stations of Ecuador have decided to transmit similar programmes that not long ago were considered of no value.

The second use of television for this project was as a media for news releases. Fundacion Natura has produced news releases once or twice a week since 1980, which are distributed to all the press agencies and television stations. The television personnel have permanently taken care of transmitting and illustrating the news with their own file material, or going out in the field to film the event or situation spoken about in the news release.

Later on, environmental subjects were used for panel discussions in television programmes, in which people from the different leading groups participated. During elections periodic programmes are specifically prepared to have the candidates discuss the most important environmental issues of the country.

Five spots were also produced for television, each one of them carrying a short message of 30 seconds, inviting the public to protect the environment. These spots are used by the television stations at their own will, with no obligation towards Fundacion Natura but also at no cost.

SOME OF THE MOST IMPORTANT RESULTS OF THE PROJECT

1. At the beginning of the second year of this project, Congress created an Ecological Commission, which was to deal with environmental legislation. It did a good job, but unfortunately the new Congress has not taken the same steps yet even though the wish has been verbally expressed.

2. The Ministry of Health, owners of a large property nearby Quito, decided to support Fundacion Natura's initiative to declare a Reserve at the top of a mountain that was a part of the property. The Reserve now is being implemented as a model scientific, educational

and recreational area, administered by Fundacion Natura.

3. The Ministry of Natural Resources has created an Environmental Department in charge of the control of the Ministry's activities.

4. The pesticides of 'The Dirty Dozen' have been banned from the importation list of Ecuador.

5. Regulations have been made for the protection of mangroves in opposition to shrimp production pools.

6. Mining enterprises will contribute with a small percentage of their income towards the protection of the environment.

7. Fundacion Natura has been able to have several governmental agencies agree on the need to produce an adequate and integrated environmental law which is being produced at the moment.

8. The electricity company has formed a technical team to produce sufficient information about watersheds that are being considered as potential for hydro-electric power.

And, what is most important, government officials are giving their full support for the new programmes presented by Natura. Of these, two must be mentioned:

A. EDUNAT II: is producing environmental education programmes for the official school system of Ecuador, providing teachers with manuals and classroom materials, and students with text books.

B. Preparation of an environmental law that will be presented to Congress.

And, last of all, trying to give citizen groups several alternatives to improve or prevent damage to their environment and think not only about their present, but about the future of the generations of Ecuadorians to come.

METHODOLOGY

A general plan was drawn up in 1979, which was later developed and reinforced by an operational plan produced and designed by Dr. Marco Encalada, a mass-media communication expert. Follow-up programmes have originated in the different stages of EDUNAT I, which have supported the most important activities of the project.

Evaluation processes have taken place all along in the project, and have allowed Fundacion Natura to re-orientate, modify or strengthen the different programmes. It has been important for the institutions and the country itself to measure the different effects produced by the project. These results have permitted Fundacion Natura to continue designing and implementing additional programmes that have become the continuation of this first experience.

Chapter Fourteen

INFLUENCING VILLAGE COMMUNITIES IN INDIA

M.A. Partha-Sarathy

I do not think it is necessary for me to explain why I have chosen the village community as the subject of my statement. Coming from a Third World, and having been involved in environmental and related problems in the Third World for many, many years, it has been easy for me to realise that the prime target in environmental concern is the village community, because it is also the primary target for exploitation, both industrial and otherwise, and is often the victim of such exploitation.

When therefore we attempt to influence the village community in environmental matters, we are teaching them, really, how to protect themselves against the assault of the urban and the industrial community.

As I speak here, my country, like some other parts of the world, has been reeling under the most severe drought that we have known in recent times. Water has receded, and disappeared from lakes and rivers. Vegetation has withered away, and died irretrievably in some places. Domestic cattle have been perishing. Water is being carried in trucks and bullock carts and on the heads of women from distant holes in the ground containing small quantities of water, to homes and to cattle sheds. Irrigation canals have been drying up and hydro-electric power stations equipped with modern machines are being threatened towards silence, because they are dependent upon that very old-fashioned commodity; in fact a primitive resource which has been something that man has had to rely upon from time immemorial - water!

In attempting to influence the village community on educating itself about the environment, we should not forget that human beings living in villages are much closer to the earth than others living in cities and in artificial environments supported by and dependent upon technology such as super buildings with controlled weather inside, super transport and super communication, not to speak of super foods processed by super technologists.

The villager lives by the earth, and dies by the earth. His waking hour is sunrise and his rest is from sunset. Rain makes or breaks his life. The nearby forest, which supplies the resilient canopy upon which rain must fall and then percolate into his field as precious water, is again a matter of life and death for him. The quality of the soil upon which he depends for his food, for his shelter and for all his other needs is more important to him than for any city dweller, whose major concern is often the greenness of the lawn in front of his porch!

We must therefore realise that when we talk to a villager about the environmental content around him and attempt to educate him about what part of the environment he must protect, what he must protect it with, we are talking to someone who already has had a rich heritage of traditional knowledge.

The question that then can be asked is, if he is so knowledgeable as all that, and if he has inherited such a valuable tradition which includes lessons in environmental protection, why is the rural environment in the Third World in such a tragic state, mangled, mauled and often irreversible destroyed. The answer is that rural communities in the Third World have not been prepared for the massive accelerating assault of technology-propelled industrialisation. It has not been prepared for the 'chemical warfare' in agriculture. It has not been prepared for the massive destruction of forests that has become necessary because of the rapid growth of the paper industry, the wood-based industry and energy consuming industries. Indeed, the rural communities have been caught unaware by this assault.

And yet, many rural communities have a culture and tradition of environmental orderliness and avoidance of resource wastage which, if harnessed properly, can be a great benefit to them today.

Let me describe what looks like a primitive example. In a typical Indian village, the family eats its food from a banana leaf which serves as a dinner plate. When the meal has been enjoyed, the housewife wraps the banana leaf around the left-overs and puts it into a garbage pail behind the house. The cow that is maintained by the house feeds upon this. This cow then gives milk and yields dung. Dung, which in sophisticated societies is classified as refuse to be discarded, is not so classified in some village communities, which use the dried cow-dung as fuel, and ash which results after the cow-dung has been burnt in the kitchen is also put back into the soil to serve an important agricultural purpose.

In modern language, this process can be called a case of excellent recycling of the resources, as well as maximum utilisation.

I am not going to harp on the philosophy that 'old is gold' and that new is something that we should look at with distrust. On the contrary, I would say that new technologies and new approaches which help agriculture, housing, transportation are all valid and relevant for use in Third World village communities. But these developments, when they are transferred to rural communities, must make sure that they do not damage more than they help. The way to achieve this is to educate and influence the village community which is to receive all these technologies in the matter of environmental safeguards and approaches that should be built into the development of these technologies into the village stream of life.

Another important consideration is the speed and degree of change that one can and should bring into a village community in the Third World. I consider this of utmost importance and it is for this reason: predictably, a dying village which has been suffering from shortage of water and wood for cooking will gladly welcome any project which will bode well all around the village and bring in lorry loads of wood from a nearby forest. It will also accept food packages, bundles of clothing and radio sets. Any human population that is desperate will reach for any straw, because it is drowning. The question is, is this the only way in which we help the village long term?

I would like to conclude by narrating the actual case of the operation of a small trust called the Rural Service Trust which a 'Swamiji' who is the head of one of India's great monasteries, and an architect of several schools for children all over the country, as well as three of us have been running. The operations of this Trust are going on even as I speak to you today. Two small villages, one with 80 families and the other with about 100 families, became the victims of severe drought. There was no fodder for the cows, no water for the fields, no fuel for cooking food, and no food to cook. Residents of these villages found that when the land went barren there was no work to do, and when there was no work to do, there was no food to eat. The Rural Service Trust adopted these two villages. The first thing we did was to go with members of the village around their own village to look at their own environmental degradation - silted ponds, and barren mounds of soil, and the dying fields and the skeletal cattle. We did not just bring loads of food and water from the cities. Instead, we determined the needs of each family and on how much a family of six could survive. Each family was asked then to name one person who would work for it. This person was given a wage of one dollar a day. We started several projects in the village. First was the de-silting of the tank - by the villagers themselves. The second was the installation of a windmill and a pump. The third was the setting-up of irrigation systems from a well to fields where fodder was planted. The fourth was the funding of ox carts owned by some families - fitted with barrels to bring water from a source ten miles away to tide over the first few weeks. Only the workforce of the village operated all these projects. Their wages of one dollar each was given as 70 cents for food and 30 cents for purchase of other necessities.

As I speak to you today, the two villages have already begun to smile. Water is flowing, cattle are feeding on fodder and have adequate water supply. We have added a new project - construction of a larger school which is an expansion of the existing one-room school, and several new homes to replace homes that are breaking up because there has been no money to maintain them.

At the most recent meeting between ourselves and the villagers of these two villages, we have been told that we will no longer be needed after a few weeks from now. This is the best news we can hear. The villagers have formed groups to ensure that the catchment area of water supply is not devastated, and that the pond does not gather silt again, and that the fuel needs of the village will not be taken from the forest, but by wood lots which have been planted around the village, and protected fiercely.

I believe we have influenced these two little villages in environmental education, of a type that has been relevant and sustainable.

An interesting footnote which further emphasises the self-support spin-off value that is inherent in these activities is that as the Swamiji and I were sitting in the village a few weeks ago putting together the workforce and deciding on who was going to be the Accountant and who the Treasurer and where we could go to collect funds, some people within the village community began to place small newspaper bundles underneath the Swamiji's chair. They were doing this unnoticeably. Most of us accepted it as part of a ritual, because in India, when a holy man appears, the devotees have a habit of paying their respects to him with a small offering or food or fruit.

However, in this case, when the meeting was over and the crowd left, and we were driving back to Bangalore, 60 miles away, I picked up the offerings to Swamiji. One can imagine how I felt when I found that inside the newspaper bundles were thousands of rupees, enough to help the village for the next several months, and donated by some of the citizens of the very same village that was in crisis. What had happened was that they had been influenced to support their own environment, and to help educate themselves and their fellow citizens on the importance of the environment to help the well-being of the village.

Index